DEFIANCE

SECRETS
OF YOUR MIDLIFE CRISIS

LOUISE L. KALLAWAY

A self-published book published by Sharanis Publishing House 2021
E | shar@sharmoore.com.au
W | www.sphbooks.com
T | 1300 32 32 12

First published in 2020 by Major Street Publishing Pty Ltd
E | info@majorstreet.com.au
W | www.majorstreet.com.au
T | +61 421 707 983

Second reprint 2021

© Louise L. Kallaway 2021

The moral rights of the author have been asserted.

A catalogue record for this book is available from the National Library of Australia

ISBN: 978-0-6487963-7-4

All rights reserved. Except as permitted under The Australian Copyright Act 1968 (for example, a fair dealing for the purposes of study, research, criticism or review), no part of this book may be reproduced, stored in a retrieval system, communicated or transmitted in any form or by any means without prior written permission. All inquiries should be made to the publisher.

Cover design by Erica Anderson, Fidget Media
Internal design by Production Works
Cover image - ChristinLola
Printed in Australia

10 9 8 7 6 5 4 3 2 1

Disclaimer: The material in this publication is in the nature of general comment only, and neither purports nor intends to be advice. Readers should not act on the basis of any matter in this publication without considering (and if appropriate taking) professional advice with due regard to their own particular circumstances. The author and publisher expressly disclaim all and any liability to any person, whether a purchaser of this publication or not, in respect of anything and the consequences of anything done or omitted to be done by any such person in reliance, whether whole or partial, upon the whole or any part of the contents of this publication.

*Understanding and overcoming the
fear of stepping away from your powerful
'need to belong' with its conformity expectations,
is possibly the maturing adult's greatest hurdle.*

I dedicate this book to everyone seeking
an emotionally independent life.

May your awesome personal power and
free will be an inspiration to others.

Acknowledgements

Once again, I wish to thank the Universe for its ongoing and hearty contribution to this second book in the 'Life Education' series. The predicaments I have found myself in so I could write from personal experience have indeed been interesting. We are a great team.

To my gorgeous daughters Paige and Suzie; your respective husbands/partners Simon and Dean; and my six grandchildren Ethan, Isabelle and Imogen, and Sophia, Blake and Isaac: thank you for your wonderful contributions to my life, helping to unravel and make more sense of my exploration into life processes and life education.

To my loyal friends, thank you for your ongoing support – specifically to Medha Murtaugh for her psychic intuitive healing; Sara for her vibrational energy healing; Monika for her ongoing astrology intel and insights; Yolla for her beautician's secrets and support for *Empowered – Secrets of Your Inner Child*; Desirea for her hairdressing skills and gorgeousness; Beverley for her magnificent eye for style and our never-ending lunches; Joan for her exquisite command of dignity and elegance; and to all those people, especially my neighbours, who make my life even more joyful. You have all contributed in your own special ways. You know who you are – thank you.

To my 'new' publisher, Sharanis Publishing House. Thank you to Shar and Russ, to all members of your professional team and for believing in my 'Life Education' series of books.

To my dedicated returning readers: on a sadder note, I feel I must let you know that my beautiful felines, Queenie and Duchess, have moved on. Ladies, I wish to thank you for the role you played as my sounding boards and personal assistants in the writing of *Empowered − Secrets of Your Inner Child.* Your memories live on. Now it is my pleasure to introduce you to my new assistant, Madelyn. My love of calico cats continues. I welcome you with an open heart. *I know* you will live up to the heavy burden left by your predecessors.

Contents

Introduction		1

Section I: Reinventing yourself — 5
1 Your invitation — 9
2 Identifying with your sense of security — 11
3 The meaning of independence and free will — 13
4 Building a courageous self-image — 15

Section II: The beginning of life processes — 21
5 Primitive programming — 25
6 Stage 1 of your development — 27
7 Childhood model fundamentals — 28
8 Disarming 'live' subconscious cords — 31

Section III: Teenage rebellion – or is it? — 51
9 Stage 2 of your ongoing development — 55
10 Being a teenager — 58
11 Rebellion vs separation — 64

Section IV: A shift in adult awareness — 73
12 Benefits of living unconsciously — 77
13 Stage 3 of your ongoing development — 83
14 Intellectual involvement with your life — 86
15 Conformity vs the individual — 90
16 Your inner 'nod of approval' — 94

Section V: The power of your emotional life — 99
17 Feelings — 103
18 Accessing your emotional life — 106
19 Positive light on anger — 112
20 Fear of rejection vs emotional independence — 118
21 Your emotional relationship with yourself — 121
22 Claiming your adult power — 125

Section VI: The chain gang — 131
23 The Establishment – who are they? — 135
24 Living within 'their' boundaries — 140
25 Unlocking your power — 143
26 Living up to your potential — 145
27 Setting conscious boundaries — 150

Section VII: More reasons for not owning your free will — 155
28 The dynamics of fear – an intellectual departure — 159
29 Know your seducers — 169
30 Liberating groundless beliefs — 175

Section VIII: Creating a more 'lived-in' life — 185
31 Putting yourself first — 189
32 Disempowering 'personal' — 191
33 Choices — 194
34 What is stopping you? — 196
35 Confronting personal beliefs — 202
36 Building your powerful arsenal — 208
37 Character-building behaviours — 212

Section IX: Lightening your emotional load — 217
38 Anger, resentments and regrets — 223
39 Naming the offenders — 227
40 'No rules' regulations — 229
41 Unlocking your patterns — 232
42 Exposing your regrets — 238
43 Self-forgiveness – a clean slate — 242

Section X: The Prison Break — 245
44 Emotional expansion – your courage shopping list — 249
45 Self-talk — 252
46 The impostor — 258
47 Fear and conformity vs emotional independence and free will — 263

Section XI: Flourishing away from 'centre' — 271
48 Reviewing your powerful new ID — 275
49 Emotional maturity — 278
50 The right to be yourself — 283
51 An independent mindset — 285
52 A tribute to the adult spirit — 287
    Coda — 289

Epilogue — 291

Thank you — 297

About the author — 299

References — 301

Introduction

Firstly, a big hello and welcome. I feel honoured and privileged to introduce you to the secrets of life processes and 'the system'. I appreciate and thank you for your trust.

Aristotle once said:

> *Give me a child until he is seven and I will show you the man.*

It has taken me 30-plus years (with myriad interruptions) and a great deal of curiosity and intrigue into life processes to unscramble and consolidate this phrase. With logical, analytical reasoning, I have been able to make sense of life processes and 'the system', and their impact on the maturing, unsuspecting adult.

If you have read my first book, *Empowered – Secrets of Your Inner Child*, you will be aware of the childhood model: your inner child's blueprint for life, put together by the time you were seven years old and brought forward into your adult life via your automatic *subconscious* responses. This model creates enormous self-doubt and power struggles when your inner child's literal, powerless beliefs about itself, its potential and life generally remain intact and unacknowledged.

It means you are living in two time zones: your automatic subconscious responses from childhood, and current time.

I have included some of the concepts from *Empowered – Secrets of Your Inner Child* to get the most out of *Defiance*. The books remain independent of each other, competent to stand alone, comfortable in their own knowledge, and complete with their powerful, life-transforming shifts in awareness that will help you to understand and make sense of yourself and your life. Have no doubt, Defiance will deliver.

★★★

I have tackled your emotional life again; it is like an ongoing internal battleground. It is, after all, the most personally empowering component in your life. It needs to be understood and conquered to allow you to progress into your personal power.

I initially considered the title *Rebellion* for this book, but somehow, the idea of rebelling seemed to always fall back into teenage territory – rebelling against conformity, authority, tribal 'ownership', the Establishment and conservativeness. Teenagers are just beginning to evolve – they are not even halfway to their freedom. They may think they are, but we know better! Teens are switching from their survival dependence on their tribal families to needing the emotional acceptance of their generation to feel okay about themselves – so they aren't independent at all, are they? They are just moving the goal posts! When you think about teens from that perspective, you can see they have a long way to go. And, may I say – no offence to the teens – it is a developmental stage. *You are supposed to rebel!* (Interestingly, I have another perspective on teens' rebellion that I will share with you in Section III.)

As you mature, you are almost on the same frequency in your ongoing development as you were in your teenage years – possibly with some extra qualifications and definitely life education and experiences to add to your worldliness.

May I say: *you are meant to be forging an independent path in this stage of your life, too.*

It is the need to belong and our emotional dependence on 'the group' that stymies the adult's progress. Conformity, for all ages and stages of our lives, produces enormous frustration. Conforming to 'the rules' of any group is unrewarding, hard work and serves no useful purpose for the maturing or mature adult; unless, of course, you are one of the office bearers or VIPs. We'll look deeper into this perspective as we progress.

As an adult, you have all the power you need to create your own identity and destiny; not the identity chosen for you as a fait accompli when you were a child, nor the need to 'fit in' with your generation – but by liberating your personal power and free will to expand and satisfy your predictable maturing needs. This is the adult's rite of passage.

Creating your own life with everything that is important to you frees you from the bitterness that often accompanies an emotionally constricted life, and from the anger, resentments and regrets that go hand in hand with self-imprisonment.

This book was written for all adult demographics with the purpose of reinforcing the need to develop our individual, inherent resources and vastness, allowing expansion of our human spirit. We should admire those people who have claimed and rejuvenated their spirit – who refuse to allow fear, conformity or the menacing 'need to belong', to run their lives any longer. They are effectively living 'I am', with their choices in plain view – amazing credits on their life's CV. This is where we are heading.

***

A few notes before we begin.

You will need a journal to jot down any extra notes; for any answers that may be more expansive than the spaces I have allocated; and for specific journal exercises.

Sometimes I have referred to 'your inner child' as 'your child' and vice versa. Those two expressions are interchangeable.

As usual, I have tried to remain as neutral as possible throughout this book.

I tend to use the masculine 'he' or 'him' rather than 'he/she' or 'him/her'. The masculine has always been accepted in this kind of position. There is no gender bias. Trust me: it makes for a much easier read.

The speed at which you move through the chapters of this book is up to you. You may like to digest this new information slowly, taking your time to answer the many questions that have been designed to reach deeply into your core; you may prefer to 'cut to the chase' with few internal interrogations; or your pace might be somewhere in between. This is your choice. To all parties, may I recommend you invest time in Section IX: Lightening your emotional load – it will be worth your time and the effort.

Lastly, should I touch on anything that causes concern for you, please consult a counsellor.

I wish you every success as you enter the realm of a *defiant* but delightful adult brat, proving there is *no real evidence to limit you*. Let's find out what a handful you really can be!

Section I
Reinventing yourself

Overview		7
Chapter 1	Your invitation	9
Chapter 2	Identifying with your sense of security	11
Chapter 3	The meaning of independence and free will	13
Chapter 4	Building a courageous self-image	15

Overview

If you have skipped the introduction, may I respectfully suggest you start there, as it is the foundation for your rite of passage.

I will be setting the tone for our journey in Chapter 1, giving you a sense of where we are heading and creating a progressive attitude that will be the theme throughout this book. We shall ascertain how deep your need for security is today in Chapter 2 and discover whether it is a major obstacle to your freedom; investigate your meaning of independence and free will in Chapter 3; and build your new, courageous, up-to-date self-image in Chapter 4. (We will circle back to Chapters 2 and 4 again later in the book, giving you the opportunity to compare and update where you are now with even more powerful insights.)

★★★

Please keep in mind that your need for more should not, in any way, be construed to mean ingratitude for everything you have achieved in your life up to this point. But … perhaps lately you have been feeling a slow burn of dissatisfaction coming to the surface; or thoughts that you *are* more, that there must *be* more, and that what you are openly and actively seeking is possible. You are now searching for strategies and more options to rejuvenate your spirit and your life – congruent with your maturing existence.

Chapter 1
Your invitation

This book has been written to take you out of the wilderness; to inspire, motivate and reignite your passion, rejuvenating your spirit.

Having devoted half my life to the study of life processes and 'the system' and their impact on the unsuspecting adult, my objective is to give you a deeper understanding as to how and why most of us, including myself, have such difficulty getting past our unconscious and subconscious obstacles. Given you have purchased a book entitled *Defiance – Secrets of Your Midlife Crisis*, you are obviously ready for change. Be assured: you have come to the right place!

Firstly, it is important to establish for the first-timers, and to re-establish for the initiated, that when I refer to your inner child, I am speaking of a child who was brought up some 30, 40, 50 or more years ago with a different set of generational values and beliefs compared to today's child. The consciousness of today's children has not begun; they are currently creating their own 'self-made' prisons. The two eras should not be confused.

Today it is all about your freedom; never against anyone, but against ingrained tribal and generational attitudes, conditioning and conformity expectations.

Mastery over your life begins when you become aware of your automatic, subconscious responses from your childhood model, and become willing to intellectually and emotionally challenge fear and its comfort zones – resulting in less concern about the need to conform, as you expand childhood emotional limitations and boundaries. The operative word here is 'overcome'.

I would like to mention at this early stage that expanding your emotional boundaries will naturally produce feelings of fear. Understand, this is your inner battle – it is the adult going against your fear and childhood model comfort zones that remain 'live' in your subconscious mind.

Have no doubt that your inherent and powerful primal 'need to belong' to your tribal family to secure your survival, and your teenage need to swap alliances for acceptance by your generation, have the potential to be huge oppressors of the maturing adult if you don't understand those constraints and where your fears are coming from.

★★★

Note: 'freedom seeking' is not always viewed in positive light, but if you are happy to go ahead and make your own choices – without the need for approval – then your life will take on feelings of exceptional freedom and exquisite free will, enabling you to create a life that is truly congruent with your more enlightened state and your maturing existence.

Chapter 2

Identifying with your sense of security

To help you progress, it is important that you have an up-to-date understanding of the meaning you give to security and your need to feel secure.

We are all born into security-conscious, self-protective behaviours which are connected to our primal will to survive and the 'need to belong' to secure our survival. Add fear to this potent cocktail and we have very sound reasons why it is difficult to move away from our programmed security-conscious behaviours. With this in mind, I invite you to ponder the questions below and write your answers in the space provided, or your journal:

How do you need to feel secure?

_____

_____

_____

_____

What do you need in your life to feel secure?

_____
_____
_____
_____

If you feel a 'need to belong' to a particular group (or groups), do you think this is coming from a sense of love, obligation or loyalty to the group? Or, is it driven by fear of their reaction if you show signs of emotional independence by choosing a different path? *Really give this question some thought. It has lots of key answers.*

_____
_____
_____
_____

Do you have a yearning for something more? Is it time to separate from the flock?

Chapter 3

The meaning of independence and free will

*If freedom of speech is the essence of democracy,
then free will must be the freedom to act.*

Independence and free will is your personal power in action. It is an acknowledgement that you are a separate entity, on your own frequency, and free to act independently with choices you make for yourself.

It is the ultimate liberation from the emotional dependence and 'need to belong' of your inner child, and your teenager's need for acceptance by your generation. Personal power is the consummate grown-up act of standing on your own; it is 'I am' in action.

**You are not attempting to liberate yourself to upset others
You are liberating yourself to make you and your life happier, healthier, more potent, dignified – free to pursue earthly endeavours without worrying about how your so-called 'non-conforming' behaviour is seen by others.**

The journey into independence is your rite of passage as an adult and an individual. The philosophy of 'personal' used in the context of this book is that it is never 'personal' against them – it is always 'personal' for you. Another important distinction: by choosing to exercise your own free will you are not fighting 'them'; you are simply choosing to walk your own path.

★★★

To add further light, I highly recommend the delightful little book Jonathan Livingston Seagull by Richard Bach. Jonathan has all the fun! The rest of the flock are quite bewildered by his actions. It will take you no time to read and you will feel the benefits and triumphs immediately from this amazing, fearless little seagull, as it creates its own magical life.

Chapter 4

Building a courageous self-image

*The nourishing thoughts you feed yourself
add power to you and your potential.*

If you have not visited your self-image previously, it will, no doubt, be seriously out of date and out of tune with who you are today. When you are still operating from your inner child's self-image, you will never be enough! In other words, you are allowing your identity, which was formed from the opinion of others from a different time zone, to validate your reality today.

What are the key words you use to describe yourself now?

_____

_____

_____

_____

_____

_____

Who you are aspiring to be? Highlight the words that resonate with you:

- powerful
- tenacious
- resourceful
- playful
- friendly
- assertive
- courageous
- kind
- honest
- thoughtful
- discerning
- grateful
- considerate
- spiritual
- intelligent
- sincere
- physically fit
- special
- individual
- generous
- analytical
- loyal
- happy
- inspiring
- passionate
- conscientious
- lovable
- optimistic
- approachable
- leader
- ingenious
- attractive
- independent
- decisive
- gracious
- stylish

Are there any other image-building words that would help you create the person you would like to be?

_____

_____

_____

Your attraction to these words shows they already have their seeds in you. It is like admiring certain qualities you see in someone: those qualities are within you, too, waiting to be recognised and acknowledged. There is a connection.

Changing your attitude towards yourself and working towards liking yourself will enable life-changing possibilities. For example, you will:

- become more involved in your life
- take better care of yourself

- no longer allow others to be more important than you
- live up to the promises you make to yourself
- no longer be intimidated by fear, moving forward or stronger personalities
- speak up on matters important to you
- become willing to explore and work with your emotional nature, your talents and strengths
- challenge your self-doubts
- recognise and work with your new choices
- allow your personal power to enter and strengthen your life.

Are there any other changes you would like to make?

_____

_____

_____

When you feel a genuine liking for yourself, your higher 'conscious' needs and consideration for yourself will begin to work in your favour! Liking yourself and believing in yourself is a breakthrough in your personal development – the catalyst for change.

It is a conscious effort to acknowledge the differences between your childhood and adult time zones! You, the adult, must allow all your up-to-date knowledge, qualifications and life education, experiences, wisdom and competence to run your life today – not the automatic, subconscious responses of your inner child's literal, powerless, dependent position, nor the opinion of others.

The following examples will show you the difference in time zone thinking:

'I don't belong anywhere'	As an adult, not needing to belong anywhere is an achievement. Belonging is no longer a requirement for survival or acceptance.
'I'm not really accepted'	As an adult, it is not necessary to be accepted. Liking yourself and self-respect are both above the need for acceptance.
'Everyone else is smarter than me'	Not everyone is smarter than you … and does it matter? You are smart in your own ways.
'I don't have choices'	When you work with intellectual reasoning, you do have choices. The list is endless – all up to you!
'No-one would want to care for me'	Caring for yourself is your adult responsibility. It is your independence at work. It is above delegation. Your life begins when you take responsibility for yourself.
'I don't deserve to be loved'	Relying on others' love leaves you vulnerable and easily played. Embracing the modern concept of self-love and self-approval is a powerful, winning attitude.

Up until now, life has been about how to fit in with others and impress those outside yourself with such things as your qualifications, the position you hold in your career, material possessions and so on. This book will help you to change that perspective. It is my job to bring awareness to the importance of your inner world, and the empowering changes that appear in your exterior world when you are working with your personal power and in your own best interests.

Just as in the above examples, you will soon see how life processes and 'the system' have been sabotaging your personal power and free will, without your knowledge or consent. I am the whistle-blower throughout this book and love dobbing them in! ☺

Section I: My challenges

Is there anything we covered in Section I that particularly challenged you? You may like to note it here so you can revisit your challenges at any time, as you continue your journey. A similar page is available at the end of each Section.

Section II

The beginning of life processes

Overview		23
Chapter 5	Primitive programming	25
Chapter 6	Stage 1 of your development	27
Chapter 7	Childhood model fundamentals	28
Chapter 8	Disarming 'live' subconscious cords	31

Overview

Your journey into personal power continues with an introduction to some of the primitive programs you were born into. These programs sculpt our lives but seem to be lost and forgotten in the vastness of time. They continue to remain potent, potentially usurping the maturing 'unconscious' adult's rite of passage.

The next two Sections will introduce you to two of the three major developmental stages in our lives:

1. childhood

2. teenage years.

These two stages create our foundations and contain many answers as to how and why the maturing adult begins to feel 'stuck', often finding it difficult to progress his personal development into stage 3.

Enjoy your 'ah-ha' moments as you delve back in time and the two earlier stages of your life.

Chapter 5

Primitive programming

How sophisticated do you think you are today?

Are you aware that your body and its systems are basically primitive? We may be less hirsute and more intellectually sophisticated than our primate cousins, but the programs that were put in place to ensure our survival in primitive times are still running in the background today. Little has changed!

Here are a few simple examples of our primitive nature:

- Our primal will to survive translates into a tribal 'need to belong' to ensure our survival.
- We are instinctual.
- Fear is programmed into our DNA, keeping us safe and helping us to survive.
- Automatic, subconscious responses from childhood are also programmed into our DNA to help us survive a hostile environment and a much shorter lifespan.
- 'Fight or flight' adrenal responses to fear helped us move out of harm's way quickly and still apply in stressful situations or when we are in unknown territory, breaking through our comfort zones.

- Our bodily functions such as our digestive system and circulation are basically primitive.
- Our life developmental stages are programmed.
- Hormonal changes in adolescence and our early teens prepare our bodies for reproduction.
- Sexual/primal urges abound to perpetuate the human race.
- Our body follows a predictable pattern of breakdown as we age.

Again, for reasons of survival, we are born with self-protective, security-conscious systems in place:

- Instincts, senses and intuition to guide us
- Fear warning us of danger
- Our emotional life making us aware of how we feel in every situation.

You can easily see from the above short lists that our primitive programming means that we are basically on autopilot. This is where the maturing adult, who is generally living a much longer lifespan today, begins to feel stuck. Would you like to note in your journal any specific areas that have come to light for you?

Throughout this book we will review the primitive programs still running today, especially those that are in our power to transcend. Specifically, we will be investigating fear and its many disguises in Chapter 28.

Chapter 6

Stage 1 of your development

Stage 1 is a major stage in everyone's childhood – the first seven years of your life.

In stage 1, you are being inducted into the ways of the world. Your inner child's experiences from birth to seven years create an unconscious model of life – a blueprint for the rest of your life. You learn about yourself, your potential and how life is supposed to be, according to a literal, instinctual, powerless, dependent, security-conscious child. This belief system is filed in your subconscious mind for future ready reference.

Once the intellectual brain takes over around age seven, you forget the unconscious beliefs of your inner child and its childhood model, but your subconscious mind remains on alert. Voila! Your programmed, automatic subconscious responses remind you what to do, how to react, what you believe and how you feel. You are now on autopilot.

Note: your developing intellectual brain is now taking charge of your life; the importance of your emotional life, now relegated to second position, is generally not acknowledged once the intellectual brain takes charge – until later. Most of us have never been taught the importance of our emotional life. More on this as we progress.

Chapter 7
Childhood model fundamentals

Think of your inner child and its childhood model as the adult's backseat driver.

The childhood model is a set of beliefs and judgements put together by a child in the first seven years of its life. As we now understand, the contents of the model are brought forward into the adult's life via automatic, subconscious responses.

Your childhood model is right-side-brain only. This model was assembled by a literal child, whose tiny world was 'personal' and serious, and whose beliefs and judgements were always survival-based and security-conscious. The intellectual brain was in its rudimentary stages of development. The model, therefore, contains no logic, reasoning or distinctions – it is totally literal!

Was there ever a suggestion that what your inner child was learning and observing would need to be reviewed to enable the adult to take responsibility for its life and its beliefs about itself? No? This was news to me, too!

Part of the reason many of us find the childhood model concept so difficult to accept is because our ego scoffs at such a suggestion – 'As if!' Our intellectual brain also has difficulty understanding how we could *still* be under the influence and displaying the subservience of a literal child. A fair rationale, too!

Our physical bodies were not expected to live more than 35 years when the formula of the childhood model was programmed into our primitive DNA. We needed a set of quick, automatic responses to accommodate such a short lifespan and survive a hostile environment. Today, with a much longer lifespan and that primitive formula still in play, your inner child's literal, powerless model, without review, is tricking you into believing *that* is all you are and *this* is all you can be.

Without intervention, your automatic, subconscious responses will continue their hold over you forever. They are the back-seat drivers of our adult lives, fear-based and emotionally contracted. Your journey into personal power and free will begins with an understanding of the childhood model.

Note: your subconscious mind does not recognise your intellect – it works with your emotions. Your inner child also works with its instincts and emotions. With such an agreeable, harmonious base, they formed an awesome relationship.

Your inner child cannot know you today – you are far beyond anything it could ever have imagined for itself. It is the one stuck in its childhood – you are not! You have choices; but, without review and intervention, your childhood model subconscious responses remain all-powerful, managing your life.

Your beliefs, whatever they are, have the power to become your successes or your failures, expanding your possibilities and opportunities or holding you back. Beliefs form a large part of your childhood model, including its imaginative ideals about how life is meant to be, how relationships should operate and how you are meant to behave. For this reason, many of the beliefs you may be basing your life upon today are out-of-date and unrealistic; they are colloquially known as baggage.

It's time to design a much bigger version of yourself, with choices and a much larger portion of the cake.

Chapter 8

Disarming 'live' subconscious cords

Your childhood model's automatic, subconscious responses have been running your life. Know this: they won't steal any more time from you!

I wrote the epic version of the childhood model and its ongoing subconscious connections in my book *Empowered – Secrets of Your Inner Child*. Now I intend to cut through 'epic', giving you a condensed version. To do this, we will look at the inner child's 'take' on various positions, the effects on the unaware adult and, finally, 'changing concepts' for the conscious adult today. Automatic, subconscious responses behave like contractual cords tying you to a set of childhood beliefs and judgements. We are about to disarm the 'live' cords and give you much bigger, conscious choices to progress your life.

Note: if the following information is new to you, may I respectfully suggest and recommend that you adopt a 'go-slow' approach, which may help to assuage any confronting feelings associated with these powerful, life-transforming insights. Trust me, there is a lot to take in all at once.

Let's begin with the most powerful and emotionally charged cord you will probably ever cut. Ready?

The need to belong

Put simply, you were born with a primal will to survive which translated into a tribal need to belong. Your inner child and mine were physically, emotionally and psychically dependent upon the family/group for our survival, safety and security. We needed to be loved and cared for. Without this basic survival need being met, we were at risk.

Today, your need to belong is no longer a survival need. Disarming the subconscious cord that binds you to your childhood tribal belonging needs is one of the most powerful, emotionally charged and courageous acts you will probably ever undertake.

I will not downplay its significance. This is often the cord that holds you back from stepping away from your inner child's emotional dependence on the family/group. Extricating yourself from your need to belong is huge – especially when it is from your family! Gulp! ☺

Sometimes the elders in the family still see you as 'their baby' and continue to control you, expecting you to conform as if time hasn't changed anything. This is part of the reason why it can be so difficult for the adult to disarm this cord. Basically, you don't want to disappoint, offend or hurt anyone; you feel a deep sense of love and gratitude to your childhood carers. Trust me, I get all of that. It gets complicated, doesn't it? Allow me to put this in a different light.

The way I rationalise this position is that you are *not* physically leaving the family, nor are you disrespecting anyone's feelings or position. Rather, you are intellectually disarming the cord to your inner child's primal and survival-based need to belong, and its emotional dependence on the family/group, enabling you to continue your evolvement. This allows a new sense of self-respect and acknowledgement for your adult self today within your family/group. You still love them, of course – that doesn't change – but it is your attitude and the way you *feel* about yourself, conduct yourself and represent yourself within that group that changes. This is your rite of passage to pursue your emotional development and your emotional independence. Continuing to conduct yourself as a child in your family/group – with no choices, fearful of owning your adult position – is no longer an option when you want to evolve. I hope this is making sense to you, and hopefully won't upset anyone's position.

The effect on the unaware adult

The adult feels caught between the two time zones, usually not understanding why. You want to forge a future for yourself but, at the same time, feel immense pressure to conform to the expectations of the family/group, as you did when you were a child. This feeling is one of the first signs that your need for emotional independence has come of age. May I say, not everyone is able to, or wants to, disarm those cords. There may be overwhelming feelings of shame, guilt and disloyalty complicating your concerns – that you don't appreciate all *they* have sacrificed for you. It becomes difficult, doesn't it? You may even find yourself making excuses for not attending some family functions.

Changing concepts

Disarming the cords to your inner child's need to belong and your emotional dependence on the family/group allows you to step away from your inner child's position and step up to a new, exciting, adult intellectual position with a feeling of equality among the older family members. This feeling of self-respect and acknowledgement of your elevated, equal position as an adult within the family – rather than a child – is what needs to happen so you can begin to make your own decisions and proceed with your life. You can now relate to your family/group on adult terms and feel a different kind of love that is borne of respect, self-respect and your 'grown-up' position and perspective. These sentiments also apply to your peer group, as we'll see later.

Depending on your circumstances, you may wish to explain to your family what you are trying to do and why you are doing it. You can clarify that it is *not against them*, ever; rather, *it's for you* – and it has everything to do with advancing yourself to the next stage in your emotional development. If you speak softly and gently with an affectionate touch, they will feel your love.

The literal child

Your inner child and mine tried hard to get it right. With only the basics to work with, they did a very good job, didn't they? They wanted so much to be affirmed. We need to thank our literal inner child for its massive contribution to our life. Can you feel its innocence, simplicity, gentleness and sweetness?

The effects on the unaware adult

The unaware adult will continue to live by the subconscious responses coming through his childhood model. That means the adult eventually begins to feel 'stuck' and powerless, frustrated and perhaps angry, but intellectually he may decide that there is nothing he can do about those new feelings. This situation is further exacerbated by his need to belong.

It is difficult and extremely frustrating trying to live by the rules and beliefs of a literal child (no disrespect to the child). No matter how well your inner child got it together, its beliefs, coming through the subconscious cords from childhood, are holding up the progress of the maturing adult. This is where anger, resentments and regrets, built up over years of feeling helpless and powerless, may finally reveal themselves as a chip on the frustrated adult's shoulder.

Changing concepts

Your intellectual brain is now fully developed – you can question, reason, discriminate and make distinctions, and intercept your automatic, subconscious responses. It is possible for you and your inner child to work successfully as a team today – triumphant as you disarm your subconscious responses/cords to the obstacles on your path to freedom. This particularly applies when you begin to push your inner child's security-conscious boundaries (comfort zones). Now that you know where your fear is coming from, you are able to acknowledge and override that fear. You are living up to your 'team' potential, affirming your inner child's position in your life.

A personal world

Your inner child's world was personal. Everything in its tiny world revolved around itself. All its judgements were based on personal beliefs. Your inner child took life and everything about itself seriously. How could it not? It was concerned about its survival, welfare and maintaining its sense of belonging for security and certainty.

The effects on the unaware adult

When the adult today still views everything from a 'personal' perspective, it becomes difficult to work with him. Living within a very narrow, single-minded, personal perspective, the adult views everything as serious, becoming scared to move away from what he knows and all his fear-based comfort zones. He needs security and certainty and finds it difficult to 'let go'. He becomes precious (or is seen as precious).

Everything is scary to the 'personal' personality. There is no lightness in this character – he is often defensive, holding tightly to his positions. We feel like we have to tippy-toe around him in case we upset him. It's a very tiny and scary place for him to live, too.

Changing concepts

When 'personal' cords are disarmed, the adult can loosen up, realising he has an enormously broad spectrum in which to work and that the childhood model subconscious responses are keeping him small, personal, self-protective and emotionally contracted – while the real world is large, negotiable and filled with possibilities and potential. We'll learn more about disempowering 'personal' in Chapter 32.

No humour about itself

Your inner child's world was based on its primal will to survive, security-consciousness, personal perspective and seriousness; so, as you could reasonably expect, there was little space available for humour. There is a distinction here: your inner child has not yet developed humour about itself; it might have laughed at other kids falling over, for example, but it couldn't laugh at itself when it fell over. Any joke or random comment made in jest about your inner child was also taken seriously with its spin. Its intellectual brain was not sufficiently developed to make such distinctions.

The effects on the unaware adult

Without humour – especially the ability to laugh at yourself – it is difficult to enjoy yourself or your relationships, or to relax into life and all its offerings. It is also hard to be around someone who is deadly serious, personal and self-protective.

Changing concepts

Incorporating humour into your life will change your life. Having the ability to see the funny side of life allows you to lighten up! Being able to laugh at yourself and see the humour in your behaviour – like watching a character on television make a mess of things – can bring new lightness into your life. Not everything has to be serious. If you can see the comedy in some of life's personal situations you will be able to enjoy more of your life, taking the seriousness out of situations that haven't worked out as well as you were hoping. Seriousness overrides joy. Humour brings it back.

Laughing – deep, hilarious belly laughing – helps you to stay alive and well. We need to take the child's seriousness out of adult equations as often as possible. Have a few movies on hand that you can watch any time you need a good laugh. I have recorded several movies for that purpose. They are so ridiculous, and even though I know what will happen next, I laugh uproariously every time! It really does make a difference. I sleep better afterwards, too!

Sensitivity

The childhood model relies on the right-side emotional brain, so it stands to reason children will be emotionally sensitive and instinctive. I am quick to say: sensitivity levels are different for every child, of course. I also make the judgement: you can't trick kids on an emotional level, because that's their language. Sensitivity is involved in the relationship they have with survival and belonging issues, too.

The effects on the unaware adult

If the adult is highly sensitive, they operate from a different emotional base to most adults. This may cause problems for the adult who is unaware or who has difficulty fitting in due to his highly sensitive nature. Twenty per cent of the population falls into this category. (If you are keen to read more on this subject, pick up Empowered – Secrets of Your Inner Child.)

Changing concepts

Personally, I can't think of any handicaps to being highly sensitive, instinctive or intuitive. However, regardless of your type, working with your emotional intelligence and your IQ will give you a much broader understanding of yourself, your relationships and your life.

Observations

Your inner child learnt about life, relationships and how it all works by observing. Children are copycats. Those observations right or wrong, true or false, good or bad – were also filed into its subconscious mind for future reference. Whichever way your inner child interpreted those observations, it believed that's the way it should be and the *only* way. Do you see any problems looming for the adult who came from a childhood where he witnessed abuse/violence or other negative beliefs and behaviours? *This is a big one, isn't it?*

The effects on the unaware adult

The unaware adult continues to repeat the negative beliefs and behaviours he observed in childhood – without review, he will automatically reproduce those scenarios that he disliked so much in his childhood, handing them on to the next generation, but unconsciously feeling powerless to change them. No doubt there would be positive, uplifting and harmless observations, too.

Changing concepts

When the adult has realised his beliefs and behaviours are a repeat of his childhood observations, he is able to change the patterns that are not in his or others' best interests. He is now living powerfully in the knowledge that he is setting new standards for himself and his family.

A world without alternative choices

Your literal inner child believed it had no alternative choices. This perspective was further reinforced by the black-or-white, right-or-wrong, either/or world it lived in.

The effects on the unaware adult

An either/or world is a difficult fit for an adult. Frustration, anger and feeling 'stuck' can be the result of living in a world that appears superficially to have no options or choices – further ammo for his resentments, anger and regrets list. The unaware adult continues to be locked into old philosophies and lacking choices, making it difficult for everyone – not only for the individual trying to live with this inflexible mindset.

Changing concepts

The adult realises that his life is filled with choices – myriad choices. In fact, he comes to the realisation that his life can be summed up by all the choices he has made for himself to date. He has lots of wriggle room to make his own decisions. The emotionally independent adult understands the benefits of grey areas in his life, resulting in a win-win for all parties. *Choices are at the heart of individual freedom.* To know it is possible to negotiate and conciliate most outcomes adds immeasurably to the adult's sense of power. There is no going back to your inner child's suffocating black-or-white world.

Conformity

Children were programmed to conform. Family and generational conformity maintained 'the order'. Fair enough, too! Unfortunately, this did not always allow the child to *feel* it was an individual. Each child is unique, but was expected to be like all the other children. Is this where we got the idea that we didn't fit in anywhere?

Conformity, when viewed analytically, also uncovers much deeper issues connected to your survival such as fitting in and being accepted. Conformity helped your inner child to feel safer and more secure. It was an unconscious reciprocal arrangement.

The effects on the unaware adult

Conformity makes the adult feel like he is living in a straitjacket. The need to conform fuels and empowers the resentments, anger and regrets list, continuing to maintain the chip on the adult's shoulder, while he remains unaware of the reasons for his feelings of disempowerment. Feelings of 'stuckness' and powerlessness shroud the adult who lives within the strictness and confines of conformity.

Changing concepts

The adult who has liberated his childhood conformity conditioning will appreciate his amazing new freedom. The adult is free, finally, to investigate life's broader possibilities without tribal, generational and societal conforming philosophies. Overriding fear and the deep issues connected with his survival and the 'need to belong' will open the world exponentially for this adult. Every adult has the right to live without conformity issues, should he wish to do so, deciding what is right for himself. It is the adult's rite of passage.

Standards and expectations

Standards and expectations are set for children, often within certain timeframes. If a child can't keep up with those standards, it will form opinions about itself that have the power to impact its self-esteem and self-worth: where deserving comes from. The child did not understand that it is not always possible to fit into those standards, or that either way, it is okay.

The effects on the unaware adult

Transitioning from childhood, feeling the effects of low self-esteem and low self-worth will chip away at the adult who goes on feeling 'not enough' or 'less than'. He may become disappointed and angry with himself for not being enough and failing to live up to the standards and expectations set by others, often 'settling' and never believing he can be more.

Changing concepts

The adult needs to review and upgrade himself intellectually and emotionally with everything he is today. Chapter 4 should change and build your new self-image. It is the 'coming of age' adult who recognises he is a single entity, able to stand alone without bowing to others' standards, expectations and approval. A whole new world is out there when the adult decides to set his own standards and expectations! The adult is the boss of himself today, not some conforming standards set when he was a literal child. Time changes everything! *This is a major one.*

Generational influences

Our inner child was moulded by the values, biases, thought patterns, attitudes and belief systems relevant to the generations who cared for him initially, and later by the beliefs and values of his peer group. Generational influences are reflected in our beliefs, which impact our behaviour as adults.

The effects on the unaware adult

When the adult remains bound by the traditional rules of a

generation, its culture and attitudes, he will continue to live a very narrow existence – not realising his power to choose for himself. Tribal and generational influences belong to the 'should' or 'should not' group of behaviours that continue to keep the unaware adult in line. The conforming adult will not go against the learnt positioning of genders either – from the choice of professions all the way down to the type of car a certain age 'should' or 'should not' be driving. He is fearful of criticism, judgement or, worst case (in his fear-based opinion), rejection.

Changing concepts

The adult can now choose for himself. He is a complete and separate entity, no longer held back by tribal and generational conditioning, any cultural patterns and old attitudes. It is another weight lifted from the resentments, anger and regrets cycle – lighting up new possibilities.

Time

The childhood model contains little, if any, reference to time. Your inner child did not comprehend the concept, relevance or importance of time.

The effects on the unaware adult

When the adult continues to live within the confines of his childhood model, he remains in the child's time zone, unaware of the enormous negative impact automatic, subconscious responses to current events have on his life. 'Time changes everything' is not in his repertoire of understanding.

Changing concepts

The adult now realises the importance of time related to everything in his life. Updating his values and beliefs – particularly about himself and his potential – reviewing old behaviours and conditioning, and liberating the childhood model automatic responses allow him to manage life much more effectively and realistically. He is taking ownership of his life.

The significance of change

This subject is completely missing in the childhood model. According to the unconscious literal child, everything it was learning would remain the same – forever. The idea of permanence gets caught up with our inner child's need for security and certainty, with fear acting as the overseer.

The effects on the unaware adult

The adult still living in its childhood model has enormous trouble accepting change of any kind. He wants 'what is' to be 'what was'. This is the child's forever belief system/thinking in action. Fear rules! The adult doesn't understand why he *feels* so fearful and, just like his inner child, usually retreats, unwilling to expand old boundaries. He is stuck in his inner child's time zone, no doubt adding to the chip on his shoulder.

Changing concepts

When the adult becomes conscious of the two time zones he has been trying to live with, he can use his intellectual brain to make substantial changes in his own favour. Personal power is in the hands of the individual who is deciding to take ownership of his life and make his own current time choices.

The inner child's identity

A child's world – its feelings about itself and its potential, its appearance, remarks about its intelligence – is related to the feedback it received and perceived from external sources. This was confirmed on a child's instinctual and emotional level by how others reacted to it or by the child's feelings towards itself when not living up to the expectations of important others. In other words, your inner child's feelings about itself and its identity, sense of importance, self-esteem and self-worth were all shaped by others, together with its spin, and filed in its subconscious mind.

The effects on the unaware adult

The adult who is still operating from his inner child's model continues to allow old opinions of himself to validate and govern his reality and who he believes he is today, creating more self-doubt and ambiguity about his potential greatness.

Changing concepts

The adult today can acknowledge all his talents, qualifications and life education, wisdom and experiences to elevate himself over and above anything his inner child thought about himself. The adult is finally admitting to himself that he can create his own security with his amazing life achievements so far. He is a work in progress and, as such, is no longer stunted by outdated, 'were they ever real?' philosophies.

People-pleasing and approval-seeking

Your inner child and mine worked hard to belong, to be cared for and to be accepted by their tribal families. People-pleasing and approval-seeking behaviours became part of the inner child's unconscious need for the intuitive feeling of affirming approval.

The effects on the unaware adult

If the adult has not realised the significance and implications of people-pleasing and approval-seeking behaviour, he will continue using his inner child's *modus operandi* without understanding or questioning why. These behaviours contribute to the adult's sense of emotional dependence, need to belong, security issues and his feelings of powerlessness and 'stuckness', as he continues to live within such subordinate positions.

Changing concepts

The adult now realises that his people-pleasing and approval-seeking behaviours can only get him so far. In extreme cases, they pave the way to becoming a doormat. The liberated adult uses a more mature, conciliatory or negotiating way of dealing with others. He now realises he has powers beyond his childhood position in every area of his life, especially in relationships, *insisting upon equality*. He is now *feeling* the power of self-approval. Well done!

There is more to the approval-seeking behaviour of your inner child than meets the eye — of course! If you feel something is missing from your life, *Empowered — Secrets of Your Inner Child* has more on affirmation and may have more answers for you.

All you need is love

Coming from the inner child's understanding, 'all you need is love' is related directly to needing love from his tribal family to survive. The child was unable to have a broader understanding of this subject.

The effects on the unaware adult

If the adult does not expand the broader meaning for 'all you need is love' into self-love, he will continue to use the child's people-pleasing and approval-seeking ways of interacting with others. This childhood model belief leaves the adult vulnerable and easily played — without understanding why. How is it possible to love others when the adult doesn't know the feeling of love for himself?

Changing concepts

When the adult begins to feel self-love and self-approval, he realises his own value. It is a major turning point in his development. Liking yourself is a significant trigger for positive change.

Fear

Fear is programmed into our DNA. Fear and your childhood model are about control and limits. They are both anti-expansion; opposite to the Universe's expansive, forward-moving and life-enhancing energy. Fear is your inner child's comfort-level dictator. Fear pressed your inner child's buttons, keeping him safe, in line and emotionally stunted. Fear always arrived in time to stop him from venturing away from his comfort zone. Every time your inner child felt fear, he retreated. Fear has its place in preparing you for physical danger, but your inner child can't make such a distinction.

The effects on the unaware adult

Fear becomes the adult's bully and boundary master when the adult is unaware of the role fear plays in his life. Fear creates the adult's emotional limitations, controlling the adult with its intimidating, manipulative strategies and tactics. Generally, the adult will not go against his fear-based boundaries without an intellectual understanding.

Changing concepts

When the adult becomes aware of the strategies fear imposes to keep him contained and safe, he can override fear with new intellectual understanding and acknowledgement. When the type of fear the adult is experiencing is questioned, he may discover that it is a perceived childhood fear rather than an actual fear. The adult understands where his old feelings of fear and powerlessness are coming from, able to assure his inner child that its need for security will be upheld, allowing the adult to override childhood fears and comfort zone boundaries – expanding adult possibilities into new horizons.

We will delve into the dynamics of fear in Chapter 28, putting it in its rightful place with intellectual acknowledgements.

Your comfort zone

Your inner child will always be fearful of moving away from what he knows, as he tries to maintain a sense of security and need for certainty. As an adult, you call it your comfort zone, but if you are still living vicariously through your childhood model, I believe it is your inner child's comfort zone that is holding up your life.

The effects on the unaware adult

The adult who doesn't understand the connection between his inner child's comfort zone and fear will continue living within the strict boundaries of his childhood model fear. He does not realise that the fear he is feeling – when he tries to push boundaries – is his inner child's fear, which continues to prevent him from taking charge and expanding his world. In effect, the two time zones are clashing. His levels of frustration and feelings of 'stuckness' will add to his anger, resentments and regrets list.

Changing concepts

This adult fully realises that the fear he feels each time he is pushing old comfort zone boundaries is fear coming through his automatic subconscious responses. The adult is now able to intellectually detach from those feelings of fear and move beyond his intimidation, allowing him to make a much bigger, happier and more satisfying life for himself.

Your belief system

The childhood model is crammed full of beliefs and judgements that potentially form the foundations of your life.

The effects on the unaware adult

If the adult has not reviewed his childhood beliefs, particularly about himself and his potential, he will lead a very frustrating life, wondering why he is finding life so difficult. Continuing to live within those confining beliefs, he will never realise his true capabilities or potential; his beliefs become his self-fulfilling prophecies. His anger, resentments and regrets list will, no doubt, continue to grow.

Changing concepts

The adult who is open to reviewing his inner child's belief system is moving towards true alignment with his adult self. He understands that there is a big world out there when his belief system is brought up-to-date with his current credentials. He is creating a powerful new image and is now free to build a new relationship with himself, his potential and his future.

Emotional dependence

Emotional dependence is a form of control in the childhood model. The 'need to belong' is an unconscious necessity for the child.

The effects on the unaware adult

The adult remains unaware that his need to belong and emotional dependence on the tribal family further exacerbate his feelings of powerlessness and intimidation. He will find it difficult, if not impossible, to stand up for himself or to say what he wants or needs and will remain emotionally stuck and powerless – again expanding his anger, resentments and regrets list.

Changing concepts

The adult who has reconciled his childhood model's relationship with both the need to belong and emotional dependence on the tribal family is taking a major step towards expanding his potential and owning his personal power. He is beginning to feel his relationship with possibilities in current time.

Self-responsibility

There is no self-responsibility in the childhood model. When you were a child, your carers were totally responsible for you. You were learning the basics, such as brushing your teeth twice a day and combing your hair. You may have been 'responsible' for one or more of your siblings, but your inner child did not understand and was not able to make the distinction between responsibility for himself and responsibility for others.

The effects on the unaware adult

The adult who remains unaware of this distinction continues to delegate and hand the baton of responsibility for himself onto someone else. There are also unconscious benefits when the adult does not take responsibility for himself and his life, which we shall review later.

As I explained in *Empowered – Secrets of Your Inner Child*, I handed the responsibility for myself over to my husband even though I was the personal assistant to the chairman of directors of a public company! I didn't connect the dots, either.

Changing concepts

The adult is now fully aware of the responsibility he has towards himself. He responds heartily to his new role. The power base of emotional independence brings him into the realm of 'nothing stopping me now!' He is making great strides, building a future for himself that lives up to everything he has been working towards. Well done! Heroic stuff! When we don't understand how powerful we really are, we waste our power.

Individuality

This is a double-edged sword; you are uniquely different to all others, but again, through your tribal need to belong, you become willing to conform, giving up some of your literally perceived 'unacceptable traits' in order to feel secure. Society also insisted on conformity to maintain 'the order'. Fair enough, too! But those positions showed little regard for individuality when *you* were a child – an important distinction.

The effects on the unaware adult

The adult who is still living within the precincts of his inner child's model will not understand that parts of his unique personality were lost to childhood conformity and his need to belong to secure his survival. Until he realises that he is an individual with his own needs, he will remain in conforming mode.

Changing concepts

The adult realises he is uniquely different to all others. He accepts his differences, takes pride in his uniqueness and likes the fact that his differences can bring freshness into his relationships – perhaps business relationships, too. He is aligned with himself and in tune with his needs, and does not require approval to live with his adult choices. Self-approval and 'I am' are at his beck and call. Excellent work!

★★★

Feeling a little confronted or overwhelmed? Trust me: I did, too! I was in my late fifties when I realised I had lived most of my life as the classic seven-year-old in the expression: 'give me a child until he is seven and I will show you the man'. Of course, I had the advantage of discovering the secrets of my inner child and its model of life gradually, but it was still very confronting and painful. In fact, I wept on and off for three consecutive days with this realisation – but my feelings of intimidation, dependence and literal beliefs all began to make sense!

Let's move forward from childhood and review the very likeable, amusing teenage stage of your development. I promise it will be more light-hearted.

Section II: My challenges

Section III
Teenage rebellion – or is it?

Overview		53
Chapter 9	Stage 2 of your ongoing development	55
Chapter 10	Being a teenager	58
Chapter 11	Rebellion vs separation	64

Overview

Teenagers often receive bad press for their apparent lack of respect, and their loud and aggressive behaviours. However, when you look at teens in a more understanding light, your beliefs may change about this developmental stage of life.

I touched on stage 2 of your development in *Empowered – Secrets of Your Inner Child*, but because that book was devoted to the inner child, the childhood model and life processes, our teen years were only briefly mentioned. Now we can investigate that stage more fully and find out if and how those years may have impacted you and your story.

Again, just like babies being born into a brand-new world, teenagers are thrown into a new stage of life with little or no experience of things to come, or how to manage the many complexities of their evolving life. Each stage of our development has a difficult set of preconceived processes to circumnavigate – hopefully we all survive, not too badly scathed.

If parents and other authority figures also thought ahead, they could relax a little more in the knowledge that almost all of us turn out okay; in fact, most of us become meek and mild! If teenagers knew this was most likely their destiny, they would be horrified!

After all, aren't they the generation who will change the world and go against the Establishment? They will never grow fat, ugly, boring and wrinkled like their parents and all those in authority, right?

I am on a mission to bring back some of your teenage 'arms crossed' body language, and hopefully rejuvenate your spirit at the same time!

Chapter 9

Stage 2 of your ongoing development

For the first time in your life, you are daring to challenge authority in a bid to shift from your childhood need to belong for survival to your teenager's need for its generation's acceptance.

Continuing your development, the second stage usually occurs sometime in your teenage years and is your first attempt to expand your emotional freedom and create a sense of your own identity. You challenge, question and sometimes conflict with your childhood conditioning and your carers' generational values and beliefs. In other words, 'we've had it with conformity. We're done with your rules!'

You begin to push the boundaries towards your emotional freedom – your right to make choices that suit your new and burgeoning independence. It is a natural progression. Unfortunately, you may have been temporarily held back in this stage by well-meaning carers, fear, financial dependence or other obstacles.

External validation, via the acceptance of your peer group, gives you a more independent sense of your value and self-acceptance. It is an important feeling: that you are fitting in; that you are okay with your generation. It is an emotional connection, reciprocal and nonverbal, rather than a survival connection. You now 'belong' with your generation.

I remember wanting to be just like my friends, who had a lot more freedom than I did. I didn't want to be different – sounds familiar, doesn't it? But my parents' controlling behaviour made me *feel* like an outcast with both parties. My VIPs were still seeing me as 'the child'. The two big frustrating issues I remember encountering in this stage of my development were not being taken seriously and not being heard.

Stage 2 of your development is a bid to gain *youthful independence over childhood dependence* and is directed towards your emotionally maturing existence and your rising need to be yourself.

It is a rite of passage and your right of passage.

★★★

The University of Otago Medical School in Dunedin, New Zealand, began the ultimate nature vs nurture test of all children born in Dunedin between 1 April 1972 and 31 March 1973. It became known as the Dunedin Study.

The Dunedin Study discovered that between the onset of puberty through to age 21, the adolescent brain is a work in progress being rewired and restructured – beginning with 'physical coordination and motor skills' in early teens, then 'emotional reactions', and finally 'judgements and control' begins its development at age 21.

The study also found that teenage offending is the norm rather than the exception. Crime is common among teens; they are looking for excitement, not thinking about consequences, since their 'judgements and control' wiring has not yet developed. Makes sense, doesn't it?

If you are interested in learning more about their discoveries, there is a fabulous award-winning documentary series by Razor Films – *Predict My Future: The Science of Us* – which includes interviews with Professor Terrie Moffitt, a lead researcher and Associate Director of the Dunedin Longitudinal Study, among others.

Stage 2 of your development, in varying degrees, openly displays your vulnerability to the world in a new role that is both frightening and liberating. Each generation has degrees of difficulty understanding some aspects of the next generation's culture, beliefs, attitudes and values; but it needs to be said: teens do not normally set out to upset or hurt anyone, especially their carers. It is not personal. Teenage acts are a preparation for entry into adulthood!

It stands to reason, when viewed in this light, that your attempt to progress from your tribal family into stage 2 was perfectly normal; and wanting to be accepted by your generation makes perfect sense, too.

Chapter 10
Being a teenager

*Our physical size defies our lack of emotional
and intellectual maturity, setting us up for expectations
far beyond our youthful possibilities.*

We have reviewed stage 1 of our development and investigated the childhood model; now it is time to align with your inner teenager and the changeover into acceptance by your generation. This was not an easy time for most of us. In fact, my difficult teenage years became the catalyst that began my study into the issues I explore in my books.

I intend to 'go to bat' for teens in this Chapter, shining a different light on their struggles and difficulties. I think the teenage years, no matter which decade, all share similar struggles particular to that stage in our lives.

Let us view that time in our lives with a new perspective. You have just left your childhood where there was *no responsibility for yourself* – then suddenly, seemingly overnight, you are expected to be 'all grown up' and aligned with the boring mindset of the Establishment! And, may I say on your teen's behalf, why would you – from what you have seen so far, your elders seem to live in a rut, boring you to tears with their unimpressive 'have tos' and 'supposed tos', their 'do as I say, not as I do' behavioural expectations, and their totally unfair and unreasonable demands on you.

So, let me make this perfectly clear:

Teenagers do not create the problems: it is the stodgy, nagging authority figures of parents and teachers that create the problems!

Stage 2 is your first step away from the tribal family. You are growing up (if they will let you!) and slowly becoming a force in your own right, realising your differences and your need to create a new identity for yourself.

Caught between the two time zones, neither child nor adult, teenagers struggle to make sense of this stage of development. You may have been confronted by any of the following, simultaneously – all with a brain that was insufficiently developed to be able to think of consequences:

- Hormones and their almost legendary imbalances
- Physical changes in appearance
- Your brain being rewired and restructured throughout your teen years and beyond
- Trying to separate yourself from a childhood image
- Trying to separate from parents, teachers and carers
- Changing over into a sexual being
- Trying to impress the opposite sex and your own sex
- Feeling pressure from parents in many different ways
- Feeling pressure from teachers and other authority figures
- Trying to decide on a course or a career path
- Feeling clumsy and awkward, even inept, in your new role
- Comparing yourself to your peer group (not always favourably)
- Trying to keep up with expected teenage images
- Betrayal in love

- Trying to fit in with your generation
- Seeking a sense of privacy
- Pressure to perform in all areas of your life
- Seeking an outlet for emotional expression.

Can you think of any others?

_____

_____

_____

_____

Having lived their lives, thus far, as the child trying to fit in and please, teenagers are looking to separate and gain some independence from their tribal families and the authority figures of their lives. They are trying to:

- run and manage their own lives
- exercise their right to make their own decisions
- exercise their right to be heard and taken seriously.

Bucking childhood conformity

We can see that there are a lot of things going on in a teenager's life – all at the same time. When you were a teen, trying to please so many people from different areas in your life may have been very demanding, placing you under enormous stress and pressure.

Now, as an adult looking back on your teenage years, you may like to look more closely at where all the pressures were coming from. This will give you a much broader and deeper understanding of this developmental stage in your life. Were you feeling pressure from:

- your family – particularly parents/carers?

- your teachers?
- your own peer group?
- yourself? (Will I ever be enough? Will I ever fit in?) Any others?

_____
_____
_____
_____

Trying to live up to everyone's expectations when you hardly know what to expect from yourself is a big ask. Remember, teens are also operating through their childhood model which has no responsibility for itself. Teens are being asked to suddenly become responsible for themselves without any real authority – they have no power to make decisions for themselves. Responsibility without commensurate authority sets them up for further exasperation and alienation from parental and other authority figures in their lives. They are fighting against the controls they felt as a child, while at the same time trying to live with the new insecurities of being accepted by their judgemental, critical peer group.

Humiliation, embarrassment and ridicule are worse than death to a teenager! They are being judged by their own generation; rejection would be the ultimate failure. Sadly, this is currently evidenced by the rate of teenage suicide and the additional emotional pressures caused by social media.

Teens will do almost anything for acceptance by their peers, even though there is an underlying 'knowing' that they are all different, but, at the same time, secretly feeling flawed somehow and not deserving their acceptance. Their reciprocal code of behaviour towards each other gives them a united front to the world.

Comparing yourself to others is never a good idea at any age, but teenagers do this constantly with their peer group. They criticise themselves harshly if they feel they are not living up to their group's approval – the same as the child when it felt it was not living up to its carers' expectations. You might recall being preoccupied with how you looked and behaved around your peers as a teen. Sometimes, worries over choosing the right course or career or passing the next exam come in at a remote second or third place compared to what they'll wear to the next party! Priorities, please!

On the surface, it seems like teenagers rebel, doesn't it? But when I go in deeper and really connect with what teenagers are being exposed to and what they are trying to achieve – even if they don't understand it themselves – I feel a deep empathy for them. Do you feel the same? Did anyone explain to you the issues you might be exposed to, and what you could be trying to achieve in this second major stage of your development? It is certainly a complicated time, and by all accounts, not the most harmonious or agreeable.

What would you like to say to your teenage self?

If you had the chance, is there anything you would say to your teenage self? Time to get out your journal and put pen to paper.

Here is what I would say to my teenage self:

> *Hi there, young Louise!*
>
> *The difficulties you were confronted with in your teens – which, by the way, is a normal stage of development – became a source of intrigue for me. I wanted to understand life processes and 'the system'. I know that your acts of independence, seen as rebellion, and the resultant feelings of alienation from the tribe were lonely for you many times, but well done! I'm so proud of you. I love you for that too! I want to give you a big hug!*

As you venture into your life, never be afraid to make a so-called 'mistake'. I believe mistakes have been viewed erroneously — they are the human version of 'trying'. Trying should be celebrated. Never forget that! When you don't try — or, to put it another way, when you are not prepared to take a considered risk — it means you have either given up, allowed fear to conduct your life or become stuck in conformity issues. You are also at liberty to change your mind and your direction to suit current circumstances. In fact, you will need plenty of flexibility to cope with all the challenges and changes that never stop. Always be proud of your independent, forward-moving attitude.

Continue to be brave. Never stop trying and never stop learning. Study your childhood model; learn about fear and the importance of your emotional life; and find out which areas in your childhood belief system are letting you down. Change or strengthen those areas and enjoy the whole process.

Always know that you are special to me, but even more so, you must feel special to yourself. Life has a way of rewarding 'special'.

Stay strong and good luck my gorgeous girl.

Would you like to live in that teenage time zone again, without this knowledge? No? Neither would I!

Chapter 11
Rebellion vs separation

I wonder who coined the term 'rebellion' when referring to the behaviour of teenagers?

As we explored in the previous Chapter, the teenage years are often chaotic and confusing – not only for parents/carers, but also for teens themselves. The more I learn about this subject, the more I believe that teenage rebellion isn't as simple as we have been taught to believe. I think the 'rebellious' teenager has been misinterpreted.

Teenagers are separating from tribal and authority strongholds; taking ownership of their lives; creating a new identity aligned with the adult they are becoming. It is a perfectly normal developmental stage.

The act of separating from previous authority figures is not personal! Most teens are not trying to upset anyone, but their change in behaviour and attitude makes them *appear* rebellious. No doubt the term 'rebellious' was coined by the Establishment, because from their point of view, that is how teens' non-conforming, rambunctious behaviour appears. Interesting, isn't it? What do you think?

It's time to look at some of the variables in a teen's life, like we did with the child in *Empowered – Secrets of Your Inner Child*. This will give us a much bigger picture of what is really going on.

Firstly, when you are a teen there is little doubt you are no longer a child. Your physical appearance has changed significantly. You are taller and beginning to take on an adult's shape and appearance. This instantly makes you more vulnerable to the pressures of family and other authority expectations.

Unfortunately, your emotional and intellectual development is still catching up to your physical appearance. This is rarely considered by the adults, contributing to further alienation. Because you are closer in size to an adult, *they* consider that you are also able to think with a fully developed adult brain – which is not possible at your age, as we discovered earlier. Physical maturity leaves you wide open to even more pressures, criticisms and expectations from all areas of jurisdiction. Most teenagers are still financially dependent upon their family, so the fit becomes even tighter and more difficult. You are now expected to behave like a grown-up, when you don't have the emotional, intellectual or financial resources to do so!

Your carers also seem to be pushing the boundaries relating to privacy and stepping into your space. It feels like they are constantly interfering in your life. Their demands seem totally excessive: keep your room tidy, get good exam results, be respectful, care for your appearance, don't be late, get out of bed, stop talking on the phone, turn the noise down and so it goes on. You seem to be in a constant battleground on the home front over something every day. Your answer is to defy or to 'drag your feet'. Do you remember your silent retorts? I will refer to this a little later.

Your peers criticise and make fun of you if you appear to be even slightly different to them. It feels like you are walking on a tightrope, doesn't it?

However, the criticism and comparisons you are receiving from the outside world are nowhere near the volume of criticisms and comparisons you are levelling at yourself. There are so many ways you aren't measuring up – in your opinion.

Your ego is working full-time in this phase of your life, too. The ego likes to think of itself as a separate individual. You know you are different from the group; you feel you are special somehow, and underneath your casual exterior you know you will be important someday – maybe you will do important work, or make a discovery, or have a vision for the world no-one else has thought of. You haven't worked the details out yet, but you know something is brewing.

You are thinking of yourself as an individual, but you also need acceptance by your peer group. Because you are separating from your tribal roots, the thought of being 100 per cent on your own at your age is scary – especially when you are not financially independent. How discombobulating!

What did you hear from others in that period of time?

_____
_____
_____
_____

What did you hear from your inner voice?

_____
_____
_____
_____
_____
_____

Did you have an identity crisis during your teenage years? Can you remember the reasons?

_____

_____

_____

When we were teens, none of us understood that our teenage brains were a work in progress, being rewired and restructured. How might your teenage experience have been different if you and the authority figures in your life had been aware of this?

_____

_____

_____

Did you choose your profession or early career path on your own? How much help did you receive? Did your parents or teachers decide for you? Was it a 'follow in the family footsteps' career path?

_____

_____

_____

Either way, are you in the right career/profession today?

_____

_____

_____

Hormones played a significant role in your teenage life. Did they lead to problems with your appearance, such as pimples, greasy skin or acne? (This is serious stuff, especially for a teen. A lot of time is spent on your appearance, further annoying the crap out of your parents. ☺)

_____
_____
_____
_____
_____

How did you express yourself? Did you have an outlet, such as belonging to a band or a sports team? How did you get rid of your excess energy?

_____
_____
_____
_____
_____

Were you given the 'After all we've done for you!' or 'Have we really wasted all that money on your education?' spiels? Do any of those phrases or words still impact you today? Spending so much time sitting studying for exams, teens often put on weight. Did you get, 'How will you ever find a husband looking like that?' (Not funny to a teenager!) Please note the most hurtful remarks:

_____
_____
_____
_____
_____

Did you make any contractual agreements with yourself when you were feeling under the hammer by your tribal family, or other authority figures? Please try to remember what they were – they may have become an obstacle for you over the years, without your awareness. An emotional outburst is almost always acknowledged with an emotional retort. The following were my retorts:

- 'I can't do anything right and I can't have anything I want, so I may as well stop trying.'
- 'You don't listen to me so why should I tell you anything?'
- 'I'll stop feeling – then nothing can hurt me!'
- 'You don't believe me when I tell you the truth; your lack of trust is making me want to rebel.'

Without realising it, my emotional retorts continued to give my power back to those people. It took me years to understand that concept and to be able to align myself and my personal power from an intellectual power base.

Please allow any of the above types of retorts to come through and note them here. This is powerful.

Was it important for your teenage self to fit in with your peer group? Note your reasons in bullet points.

_____
_____
_____
_____
_____
_____
_____

Dwell on your answers to the last two questions, especially if you think they may have created an obstacle for your emotional expansion and free will. Do you now see teenage rebellion in new light?

Section III: My challenges

Section IV

A shift in adult awareness

Overview		75
Chapter 12	Benefits of living unconsciously	77
Chapter 13	Stage 3 of your ongoing development	83
Chapter 14	Intellectual involvement with your life	86
Chapter 15	Rebellion vs separation	90
Chapter 16	Your inner 'nod of approval'	94

Overview

In this Section, we are once again going back to basics to pinpoint why it's easier to live our lives unconsciously, and the reasons how and why we *feel* powerless when living through the childhood model and our teen's need for generational acceptance.

As we've learned, the significant players in the first two developmental stages are:

- the need to belong – tribal and generational
- fear of abandonment – a primal fear – and security issues
- group acceptance – the need to fit in and be approved of
- group dependence to feel supported and okay about ourselves
- conformity issues.

Note that emotional independence does not play a role in stages 1 and 2. Generally, we cannot be emotionally independent and still fit into 'the group' and its culture, expectations and conformity issues. *Ah-ha!*

We'll take a look at consciousness and what that means to the adult today.

Chapter 15 explores the relationship between conformity and you, the individual, revealing the antagonists to your freedom today; and Chapter 16 wraps this Section up, with your inner 'nod of approval'.

Chapter 12

Benefits of living unconsciously

Living your life in the unconscious world of your inner child is an easier option, but it separates you from your personal power. It is a double-edged sword.

When we think about it, it's easy to see why we are tempted to live life unconsciously. On the surface it has many benefits:

- You never have to take an assertive role in your life.
- You can continue to blame without ever taking responsibility for your part in the scenario.
- You can remain the support, never taking a leadership role.
- You don't have to take *any* risks or push childhood model comfort zones.
- You can continue to avoid and stay out of the spotlight, safe and secure.
- You never have to stand on your own or speak up on matters important to you.

- You don't have to step out and away from tribal and generational acceptance.
- You never have to chart new territory for yourself or your potential.
- You don't have to review your values, beliefs or attitudes.
- You can avoid introspection, continuing to live through automatic subconscious responses from your childhood model belief system.

Can you think of any other benefits? There's bound to be more.

_____

_____

_____

_____

_____

_____

Of course, it is possible to live the whole of your life through the subconscious responses of your childhood model belief system. In fact, most people do – never fully realising their potential or what it feels like to own their personal power or enjoy their free will.

Now it's time to check out what living in your inner child's comfort zone *feels* like and *sounds* like. When your responses remain unexamined, they act as a barrier between you and your personal power. To know how you are responding to certain circumstances will give you a much clearer indication of where you may be in your emotional development today.

Now let us take a closer look at your possible responses and find out if they sound like your inner child's responses to certain situations, the responses of a frustrated and unconscious adult, or straight out fear. More choices! It's so interesting, isn't it?

- **Do you prefer to stay in your comfort/safety zone?**

    Safe response: 'Well, yes. It helps to eliminate some of my anxiety. It feels safer somehow. I don't want to step outside my safe zone. How will I cope? What if I fail? Anyway, it's okay here.'

- **Do you tend to complain about things not working out for you?**

    Safe response: 'Of course. Doesn't everyone? Things just happen. It's not my fault! My efforts don't seem to make much difference. I try to accept things the way they are.'

- **Have you become indifferent about yourself and others?**

    Safe response: 'Yes, maybe. I know it feels better when I don't rock the boat. I don't feel so anxious, either. Nobody listens anyway. I end up making a fool of myself. Nothing really changes.'

- **Do you fear self-expression?**

    Safe response: 'Well ... yes. I hate drawing attention to myself. I hate being in the spotlight – it's embarrassing. I don't have the confidence – and, anyway, I'm happy to listen and watch others. I don't want to risk embarrassment if my contribution is rejected.'

- **Do you remain silent, never questioning anything?**

    Safe response: 'Keeping the peace is a lot easier. I'd rather be the nice guy and fit in.'

- **Have you ever questioned the beliefs and values you were brought up with?**

    Safe response: 'I haven't really thought about them. I don't want to risk upsetting any members of my family or close friends; there are enough hassles out there. I like being agreeable. It suits me … it suits everyone.'

- **Do you stay as 'sweet as pie', hanging on to your anger and resentments?**

    Safe response: 'Firstly, let me make this perfectly clear: I don't have issues! I like to appear nice and agreeable. No good upsetting anyone, is there? But, sometimes, things r-e-a-l-l-y get to me!' *(Busted!)*

- **Do you fear change?**

    Safe response: 'Well, yes. I don't push boundaries! I don't really need to challenge myself or others. I'm pretty much okay with things the way they are … most of the time.'

- **Do you constantly seek the company of others?**

    Safe response: 'Of course. Isn't that what life is all about? My loved ones fill in the gaps. I would be lost without my family and friends. I don't like being on my own.'

- **Do you make concessions justifying or excusing people's behaviours?**

    Safe response: 'Well, I suppose so. Everyone does it. Everyone's stressed. We all have bad days. No use making a fuss, is there?'

- **Do you use rebellion as a way of dealing with your life?**

    Safe response: 'Sometimes. Why not? I feel pressure and I can't handle it. I figure if I act tough maybe people will leave me alone. I don't need their constant hassling!'

Can you see how most, if not all of the above responses are linked to your child's survival-based and belonging strategies? Are you surprised? I know I was!

Did you see any responses or patterns you use today? Would you like to note them?

All these responses boil down to not wanting to take a risk, fearing that self-exposure may lead to ridicule or embarrassment, and not wanting to rock the boat. Does it sound like 'settling' to you? Overall, avoidance is the winner! It was my favourite for a long time. But, you know, avoidance goes nowhere and it makes you feel bad. It's like you've missed an opportunity to own up to what you are really feeling or what is important to you. It feels awkward; you feel awkward. These are the safe responses of your inner child.

When you continue to live behind the security gates of your childhood model, you think you've dodged the bullet, but it leaves you *feeling* powerless. Let's go deeper.

You, the adult, are not powerless. But, if you remain in the emotional dependence and unconsciousness of your inner child and its model – you feel powerless!

Let's dig into this proposition a little further.

You, the adult, have no such emotionally dependent boundaries. You are now physically independent and able to use your fully developed brain to give you an intellectual edge over your childhood model. It's your inner child that continues to live in its tiny security-conscious world via your subconscious responses that is preventing you, the unconscious adult, from claiming a much bigger and more satisfying life in this time zone.

It is a shift in your awareness and a change in your attitude that allows you to embrace your burgeoning personal power.

Chapter 13

Stage 3 of your ongoing development

We passionately wish to claim our lives.

I believe most of us do what we are 'supposed' to do, what we have been taught to do – taking on the responsibilities of marriage, children, careers, mortgages and so on without question. But one day, the fit becomes too tight! Simply, it is too hard to live in this tiny space any longer. You long to stretch your wings! This is a sign that your emotional development is ready to advance.

In other words, your emotional life wants to catch up with her big brothers: your intellect and physical size. She wants to expand your inner child's fear-based comfort zones.

Stage 3 is the adult's predictable maturing need for independence and free will vs the need to belong to either group with their conformity issues. This stage is often referred to as the midlife crisis.

As we touched on in Chapter 7, when the primitive system of subconscious responses was introduced into our DNA, we were not expected to live beyond 35 years. Today, with the development of our intellectual brain and a much longer lifespan, the unconscious maturing adult will be feeling 'stuck'. This feeling is emotional 'stuckness' where you are:

- stuck in your inner child's belief system
- stuck in fear-based comfort zones
- stuck in old patterns, attitudes and behaviours
- stuck in need-to-belong conformity expectations
- stuck in emotional dependence issues
- stuck in childhood coping behaviours such as avoidance and blaming
- stuck in your inner child's yes-or-no, either/or world
- stuck in your need for others' acceptance rather than self-acceptance
- stuck in and adding to your anger, resentments and regrets
- stuck in powerlessness.

If your emotional life remains emaciated or unacknowledged, it will not be possible for you to evolve with only your IQ. You have never been taught the importance and value of your emotional life. I believe most problems in our lives are emotionally based. Trust that the feelings you don't or won't acknowledge rule your life and they will get your attention in any way they can; sometimes through addictive behaviours such as alcohol, drug or food issues.

Stage 3 is just as confronting as the previous two stages, but this stage often seems to require a catalyst or a motivator to get you started and wake you up! Let's try to move into stage 3 without the need for a severe, life-changing prompt. There will still no doubt be a prompt, but a minor one will suffice. Either way, claiming emotional freedom is your reward.

You are entering real life now. You are becoming the chameleon-like adult, willing to adapt, change and respond to your conscious adult needs. Life will appear fairer as you look through your newly created skylight into the possibilities. You are now in the conscious zone.

Chapter 14
Intellectual involvement with your life

Consciousness, in this instance, is the realisation that there is more. It is your evolution into reality; a willingness to embrace your personal power and free will.

In retrospect, it disturbs me that I didn't give any thought to the crossover between childhood and adult life and what that really means in a broader sense. My age simply placed me there. Is this the same for you?

Without exception, we all have something (or a lot of things) we bring from childhood into our adult lives. If your inner child thinks it got a raw deal, you will most likely be carrying those wounds in the form of anger, resentments and regrets, defensive behaviours or a chip on your shoulder. This will, no doubt, be affecting your attitude and everything about you: your health, your opportunities and your potential.

You are so much smarter, wiser and more intelligent today than you were as a child, and you have a lot more life experience and life education to call upon. So, no more victim mentality – it is not allowed! A victim mentality locks you into a never-ending cycle of helplessness, powerlessness and, eventually, bitterness.

Blaming and avoidance weakens your position, too. No more scapegoating! You don't need such fallback positions. You are heading towards 'I am'. You are searching for a bigger range of options – an adult range of options. All the life experiences and life education you have been building and gathering over the years are about to be put to work.

When you were younger you didn't know, nor did you understand, that fear, your need to belong and emotional dependence on the groups would become your self-made prison – or that they had the power to usurp your continuing development.

It's time to turn the tables. You no longer need your inner child – or anyone else, for that matter – bossing you around. You certainly don't need permission to evolve. You are now the adult, taking charge and defying the limitations of stage 1 and 2 of your development. It's almost scary to think how powerful you really are when you are no longer held back by emotional dependence on any group. It's time to check out what has been happening in your life lately and become involved in your life on an intellectual level.

You have come a long way since you were a child. You know how it works! You have worked hard, worked within all the beliefs and conforming behaviours of your conditioning. You know how to live in the world today, how to present yourself, how to behave. You are now a physically independent adult, most likely earning your own income, financing your commitments, supporting yourself and possibly others.

Lately you often feel like a little kid, mildly concerned about what people may think of you and still feeling a need for outside acceptance; wondering whether you'll be able to handle the next situation that comes your way or whether you can continue to live up to the standards society expects of you.

You know that sometimes, especially lately, you have felt a trifle overwhelmed, like you did when you were a child, and wonder where that's coming from.

And, you are willing to admit, your life could be better! You've been thinking recently, 'Surely there is more to life, more to me. This can't be all there is!' You have never felt like this before; this is a new experience for you. Congratulations! You are evolving!

Your catalyst for change

To make the move into consciousness, it seems you need a catalyst or a motivator. It's always personal. Can you pinpoint it? Maybe you have been feeling that something is missing from your life, or maybe you've been thinking 'where to from here?'. Perhaps there has been a huge disappointment: maybe the loss of a job, loss of a dream or a love affair that hasn't worked out for you. Perhaps you haven't been feeling well lately. Regardless, you are surprised by its impact and the resultant intense feelings of insecurity and confusion.

Sometimes those types of influences disguise themselves as depression. Is your catalyst depression? I once read that depression is anger turned inwards. It appears as a 'soft feeling' – not the loud and aggressive version that is usually associated with anger, but one that shrouds you like a heavy fog. This soft anger or depression can leave you feeling despondent, dejected and powerless, but most of all self-blaming/self-flagellating.

I'm not sure everything in your life needs to feel heavy to move you forward. The point is, in this instance, you need to blame something – make the most of it! Blaming has passed its use-by date!

Can you identify the culprit, or the one 'most likely'?

_____

_____

_____

_____

_____

The act of giving anything power over you belongs to the past. Whatever your catalyst or motivator, it needs to be acknowledged, together with your feelings. This will discharge and disconnect its power over you. You are becoming the 'mover and shaker' of your life – defying powerlessness!

As Marianne Williamson says in her book *A Return to Love:*

> *Our deepest fear is not that we are inadequate. Our deepest fear is that we are powerful beyond measure. It is our light, not our darkness that most frightens us. We ask ourselves, 'Who am I to be brilliant, gorgeous, talented, fabulous?' Actually, who are you not to be?*

Chapter 15

Conformity vs the individual

We all like to be cared for, but realise this: when you take responsibility for yourself and everything about your life, you will care for yourself better than anyone.

Your freedom is based upon liking yourself and your right to make individual choices, above conformity issues. When you let 'the group' set your emotional boundaries, your life will not evolve.

Fear, your need to belong and the group's conformity expectations are the antagonists of freedom – they are the adult's unconscious bullies!

Your inner child and its need to be cared for, and your teenager's need for emotional acceptance by its peer group, conflict with your need for personal freedom today. Of course, conformity was necessary in stages 1 and 2 of your development; but in stage 3, your need to belong to any group has the potential to squash your individual freedom.

Fear is a major player when you begin to make transitional changes in your life that are more suited to your adult position. Effectively, you are on a mission to expose the areas of your life where you may knuckle under, avoid, blame, remain silent or allow fear to compromise your need to expand your emotional boundaries in favour of your personal power and free will.

In other words, stage 3 is where you become the real you with no strings to the outside world – no more needing to belong to any stage in your development, level or group. Learning to be on your own will help you to *'overcome'*. Being comfortable in your own company without constantly needing to be around others is good for your spirit and your self-esteem. It also reinforces the fact that you are a separate, single entity and that you are okay on your own. It is another form of self-reliance.

Remember, you are not employing your free will to aggravate anyone – you are simply pleasing yourself. This is the act of a maturing adult who has realised his personal power.

Adult free will is a collaborative effort between intellectual intelligence and emotional independence. It is yin/yang – the Chinese complete. Our intellectual intelligence helps us to formulate our prison break; our emotional independence determines how far we will push fear-based boundaries and open our lives to limitless opportunities. Emotional independence is your power base.

Conformity is built into us as children, for good reasons. There it remains until we realise how often conformity raises its head, reminding us with fear that we are pushing (childhood) boundaries and we need to stay safe and secure within the precincts of 'approval'. As I said previously: life is about overcoming – that's the challenge. This one is right up there! Once again, it seems anything worthwhile can't be half-hearted. How are you feeling? Okay so far?

I must say, conformity has been the bane of my life. The expectation to fit in, to belong and to be accepted has become almost a bullying tactic, dictating to others (most often silently) how they should live their lives. What is so difficult about allowing others to live their own lives? Who decided this for us? Some old fogeys? Who upholds this tradition? You will have an opportunity to answer those questions later.

Bottom line: do you think it's okay to live *all* your life as a child – under the strict hand of conformity and the rules you will probably never have an opportunity to change? Do you think that we are not responsible for anything and that we are no more than robots living as we were instructed and conditioned to live as children?

Note: If your decision to live your life independently is seen as 'personal' by anyone, remember that the stage in *their* development is on display too.

Our emotional life + our beliefs = our behaviours

Behaviour gives us away. The stage in our personal development is easily identified by how we behave. Let 'them' know if they continue to view your behaviour personally that it is not personal *against* them – it is a choice to live 'on par' with your maturing life.

It's all about feeling good about yourself and your life. There's no such thing as selfish as you age, either – you've already put in the hard yards and worked with life. Now you are taking charge and deciding how you want life to work for you.

Using free will quietly, with dignity and grace, is a choice. I would love for you to know what it feels like to go against ingrained thinking and attitudes and build a bespoke life for yourself. Expanding your emotional boundaries and going against the pack is not always easy but trust me: it is worth the effort. You are becoming a fully-fledged delightful adult brat – so, think big!

To bring you back to yourself – what are your reasons for reading *Defiance*?

Chapter 16

Your inner 'nod of approval'

Moving into the higher realm of liking your adult self today will be your consummate catalyst for change.

Liking the adult version of you is the beginning of your new life. Until you change your attitude towards yourself and your life, how is it possible to like yourself and, further, how is it possible to believe in yourself? Liking yourself is aligned with personal power.

Your new attitude will have huge benefits, impacting on and reshaping all the areas in your life that you feel are unsatisfactory. It will create a new involvement with yourself. You will become more and more willing to push once inflexible childhood model boundaries as you embark on your emotional independence. You will sense old childhood barriers begin to weaken as you become more proactive on behalf of your adult self. Action manifests personal power.

I have learnt that my first reaction to something – especially something that appears to ask too much of me – is almost always my inner child's reaction! If you are not aware of this possibility, you will take your immediate reaction or response to mean, 'I am not up to it'. Most of us think we are not up to whatever the next step is for us.

In fact, my inner child's reaction to me writing my first book almost shut the book down before I even started! The feeling reminded me of fear, but I didn't feel nervous about the idea; there was no anxiety. It was more like a threat to my inner child's sense of security — what if it failed, what if it embarrassed itself? It would be out of its comfort zone. Then, what would it do? Your inner child will always view everything literally, seriously and from a personal perspective. It is your inner child that will be out of its comfort zone, if or when you take the next step.

Unveiling your awesome power

Childhood model constraints always leave the adult feeling compromised and powerless. The childhood model contains few, if any, experiences or examples of self-reliance, self-responsibility or emotional independence. Those childhood model feelings of powerlessness and helplessness interfere with the manifestation of your personal power. So, before you can move forward, you need to understand how you feel helpless or powerless.

Let's take a look at how the seemingly disparate positions of not liking your adult self today and your inner child's feelings of powerlessness fit together. The following examples are presented to show you how my feelings of powerlessness contributed to the dislike I felt towards myself, when I was living vicariously through my inner child's model. I didn't like myself:

- when I felt helpless or powerless
- when I felt embarrassed, humiliated, guilty or shamed
- when I was financially dependent
- when I felt beholden to someone
- when I acted in opposition to myself in order to fit in
- when I felt intimidated and didn't stand up for myself or say what I needed to say around important others
- when I felt I wasn't enough

- when I allowed fear of offending someone to keep me emotionally contracted
- when I didn't end relationships that were no longer working for me because I felt too emotionally intimidated to sever the ties or didn't want to be on my own
- when I felt used or taken for granted but I didn't say anything
- when I automatically made someone else more important than me and I didn't understand why.

Would you like to add any that may have come to light for you?

_____
_____
_____
_____
_____
_____

You will find even more of your answers will come to light for you in Section IX: Lightening your emotional load. But no peeping! There is a lot more to cover in the meantime.

Section IV: My challenges

Section V

The power of your emotional life

Overview		101
Chapter 17	Feelings	103
Chapter 18	Accessing your emotional life	106
Chapter 19	Positive light on anger	112
Chapter 20	Fear of rejection vs emotional independence	118
Chapter 21	Your emotional relationship with yourself	121
Chapter 22	Claiming your adult power	125

Overview

It is your emotional life that decides how you are feeling and where you stand with yourself – whether you are 'down' or feeling emotionally nourished with a sense of emotional wellbeing. It is your emotional life, too – emotional expression, emotional expansion and, ultimately, emotional independence – that will lead to the unveiling of your personal power and free will. Never underestimate its importance in your life. Your emotional life needs equality with her counterpart – your intellect.

Chapters on the importance of feelings, how to access your emotional life and your emotional relationship with yourself are included in this Section. Combined, they add heartily to your free will destination. Bottom line: your emotional life needs to be understood and acknowledged or it will continue to manage your life.

Only when you rationalise and acknowledge the burden of responsibility you have towards yourself – the right to be yourself and make decisions in favour of your emotional freedom above anything else – can you feel your personal power come to life. We must be prepared to use adult moments of *defiance* to progress our lives.

It takes guts and determination to go against fear and conformity – tribal expectations and your generation's rules. Don't scoff at the few people who do – they should be applauded!

Think about how your life will be different when you are working with and living an emotionally independent and liberated life.

Now, let's peel back more layers, moving closer to your freedom.

Chapter 17
Feelings

*Your mission is to recognise and acknowledge
your feelings and take control of your emotional life.*

I know it's easier not to feel; but when you try to live your life without paying attention to your feelings, you lose contact with yourself, putting an even wider gap between you, your personal power and an evolving life.

Your feelings are the closest and most intimate part of who you are. Your feelings are unique to you, separating how you feel from everyone else. If someone or something can hurt your feelings, imagine how hurt your feelings must be if you have ignored them for years. (If your ego has just scoffed at my last remark, and you have chosen to ignore your feelings till now, they must be feeling just as frustrated and 'stuck' as you were!) The feelings you don't or won't acknowledge rule your life. As mentioned earlier: they will get your attention in other ways.

Avoiding, neglecting or ignoring your feelings does not make them go away. Instead, they gather strength in numbers, unbalancing your sense of wellbeing and persisting without your acknowledgement.

Your feelings decide what you feel. They are all-powerful. Effectively, they are your personal radar; your honesty with yourself. They are your constant reality check, letting you know how and what you are feeling and how you are coping with what is happening in your life.

If you have spent your life ignoring your feelings, their weight can unbalance and eventually disturb your emotional wellbeing. Where do feelings go when they are ignored? They live in your body; in their preferred organs such as your liver or spleen. Choosing not to acknowledge your feelings would be like leaving a program running on your computer that is never switched off. Imagine how many unfinished programs would be running after many years of ignoring them!

To give you a greater understanding of how important your feelings are to your wellbeing and the role they play in your life, here are some of the promises your feelings make to you.

They:

- are 100 per cent on your side
- are candid and honest with you
- protect you by making you aware of your current situation
- add meaning to your life
- are intuitive and exclusive to you
- are always biased towards your best interests
- are reliable
- are the balance in your life
- contain warnings, including anger and fear
- don't justify circumstances or what is happening

- allow softness and compassion for yourself and others
- are your servants
- are your reality check.

Tuning in to your feelings is empowering. They will expand your world. They are the foundations of your new power base. It's about getting to a higher state. Your feelings will help you get there.

Chapter 18
Accessing your emotional life

You are about to form an alliance with your feelings. Feelings belong to the social realm of your life, wanting to be recognised and acknowledged, keeping you aware of what's happening in your inner world and how you are coping with your outer world.

Your feelings need your acknowledgement for all the work they do – the same way you like to be acknowledged for all the work you do! Acknowledgement includes all your feelings – not just the delightful ones. Acknowledging your feelings plays an important role in:

- your state of physical and mental health
- your general and emotional wellbeing
- your motivation
- your energy levels.

I would like to make an important distinction:

You are not your feelings! Feelings create the emotions you are experiencing.

So, how do you gain access to this information?

You pay attention, you stay awake, you become aware. You work with your feelings; you become purposely conscious.

Recognising and acknowledging your current emotional state is the key. This must surely be one of the sweetest and best-kept secrets of an empowered life.

I discovered I was seriously out of touch with my feelings; I hadn't realised their significance or their importance in my life. When you ask yourself regularly, 'What am I feeling?', you are bringing your attention back to yourself and becoming aware of the many changes in your emotional connections with yourself. You are acknowledging your emotional life and staying in tune and aware of how you are coping in your daily life and your current situation.

Your feelings are your constant companions – guiding, alerting and intuiting you – making you aware of your connection with yourself, others and the outside world and your position within those spheres.

Initially, don't be surprised if you don't know what you are feeling. With practice, you will recognise your feelings quickly as you align with their intelligence. 'What am I feeling?' is a treasure trove key opening a whole new world for you.

What am I feeling?

Let's start here. You will try this exercise because nothing else has worked and you want to be free to enjoy your life and maybe better health. Think of it as a guessing game. Begin to guess – what is the feeling you are experiencing?

I'm feeling:

_____

_____

_____

Keep guessing. I'm feeling:

_____

_____

_____

You may have to ask the question several times before you have guessed correctly. When you do, you will feel moved; you will soften or resonate with that feeling. You have recognised and admitted to the feeling you are experiencing. Now you can acknowledge it by saying:

'I'm feeling _____' (whatever it is).

Then, let it go. Sometimes you may wish to sit with the feeling a little longer, but acknowledgement is all it wants from you. Your feelings are no different to you. They want your recognition and acknowledgment, as I have said previously, for all the work they do for you. And fair enough, too!

Sudden unexpected fearful emotional reactions

If working with your feelings is new for you, please stay alert to sudden, unexpected emotional reactions. These can vary from a vague sense of uneasiness to high-intensity overwhelm. They are most likely your inner child's fear-based reaction or response to your current situation. If you are having such a reaction, can you pinpoint why you are suddenly feeling this way?

I discovered that sudden, unexpected fearful reactions are almost always our inner child's feelings coming through the subconscious mind. As a child, fear set the boundaries for unfamiliar, challenging situations or a new experience. Your inner child usually retreated. It is your inner child that is feeling the boundaries of its comfort zone – not you, the adult! *This is another major distinction.*

Watch how your inner child's emotional reactions to situations that push it to the edge of its comfort zone still have the power to turn you away from moving forward, too – when you are unaware of their origins. Remember: your childhood model is about security and certainty.

When you, the adult, push old childhood model comfort zone boundaries, you will feel fear-based reactions. It is almost guaranteed!

As adults, we need new ways to intellectually respond to our childhood model fear-based reactions, otherwise we think we are not up to the task of dealing with whatever is provoking that feeling.

Because you are now aware of how security-conscious and tentative your inner child really is, you may like to use the following intellectual response to reassure yourself and pacify your anxious inner child when you are experiencing such reactions:

'I know you are feeling anxious, but I'm taking charge and you don't have to feel frightened anymore. I won't leave you; I'll keep you safe. We're a team now. Let's move forward together, past your old comfort zones, and find out what life has to offer when we do. I promise I will take care of you.'

Now, let's look at two examples of sudden, unexpected fearful emotional reactions. (I might add here: fear loves surprises such as a new situation or an unexpected outcome. It really is a menace, isn't it?)

Feeling anxious, uneasy or stressed?

When you suddenly feel anxious, uneasy or stressed for no apparent reason, those feelings are most likely coming through your subconscious mind because your inner child is again feeling that it's out of its comfort zone with your current circumstances or position. Is your inner child feeling it can't cope, may fail or, worse, embarrass or humiliate itself in front of others if it tries something new? We can only guess the reasons.

Now you can acknowledge your inner child's fearful emotional reaction, pacifying and reassuring your anxious inner child with the example response above, enabling you to direct new, powerful, intellectual and positive emotional responses. You are, in effect, expanding your comfort zone. Another triumph for your personal power.

Feeling overwhelmed?

When you suddenly feel overwhelmed or panicky, you can be sure that your current situation is more than likely pressing your inner child's buttons. Sit back for a moment and breathe. Is it a feeling of 'I can't do this' or 'I'm not up to this'? Or do you feel as though you're not ready yet; you are too inexperienced, too untrained, too uneducated or simply too fearful to have a go? Or, maybe it's more aligned to the feeling of embarrassment or humiliation.

You now know, none of those reasons apply to you today. Simmer the situation down with your intellectual brain. You are moving away from your inner child's fear and comfort zones, using your intellect to convey to your fearful, anxious inner child that there is nothing you can't handle together now! You are the one in charge of overwhelm and panic, creating new horizons for both of you.

These exercises may take some practice but remember: every day presents you with new opportunities and new beginnings.

I wish I had understood my reactions to fear. Armed with this incredible knowledge, I could have lived a much bigger and more powerful life and not been so intimidated by some circumstances and my inner child's feelings of powerlessness. More on fear later.

When you become the master of your emotional life, you will feel a definite shift in your awareness and connection with your power base.

Chapter 19
Positive light on anger

Imagine how anger must feel after years of being ignored, pushed down and silenced every time it put up its hand for recognition. It can be likened to a time bomb or a loaded gun: volatile and ready to explode or implode in unexpected and frightening ways. We've all seen those types of incidents on the six o'clock news, haven't we?

What is anger? I believe anger is connected to your ego. Feelings of anger are stirred when your ego, which likes to feel superior and separate, instinctively feels and believes you have been ignored, not been taken seriously, have been treated unfairly or have been *generally disrespected*. The feeling of anger is in response to an outside source. When you consider the ego is concerned with its image and how it is seen by the exterior world, this analysis makes perfect sense.

I read somewhere that anger may be related to a sense of personal loss of some kind, including a presumed or theoretical loss such as missing out on a promotion. 'More disrespect! How could this happen after I worked so hard?' You can sense anger in this scenario, can't you? Anger can also have its roots in controlling and vindictive behaviour.

To set the scene, let's look at some examples of how anger may enter your life (along with being ignored, not taken seriously treated unfairly or generally disrespected). Anger can present when you:

- are unwilling to accept a ruling – it should be your way
- refuse to acknowledge your feelings of anger
- experience trust issues or feelings of betrayal
- have experienced a negative defining moment, or a defining moment that has left you churning, despondent or feeling diminished
- lose something or someone important to you
- feel you have been played
- experience unrequited love
- have a regret you can't forget
- feel used, abandoned or rejected by an important other
- experience a loss of face
- have a realisation of some kind
- experience an embarrassing or humiliating moment
- relied on a promise of some kind that has not come to fruition
- have lost your job or your home
- have separated or divorced
- feel you are in a no-win situation (for example, worrying that you may lose an important relationship if you speak up).

Any others?

_____
_____
_____

Anger may also be felt and expressed in many other forms and disguises:

- total frustration
- inappropriate expression (such as verbal abuse)
- churning
- irritability
- bullying and controlling behaviours
- over-sweetness
- complaining
- belittling
- negativity
- a victim response
- jealousy
- judging and criticising
- spitefulness
- passive aggressive behaviour
- bitterness
- sarcasm
- depression (soft anger turned inwards)
- impatience
- defeat or exasperation
- a change in mood or a sense of uneasiness in the company of a particular person.

Any others?

_____

_____

_____

Now, let's turn the tables and find out how anger may act out when it remains unacknowledged.

Anger is energy that needs plenty of space and attention. It needs to blow off steam. It does not like to be ignored or cooped up! Anger becomes furious when you don't or won't acknowledge its presence, pretending you are fine. You are effectively rejecting your ego's wisdom. Anger is a force! It has the ability to commit murder! It is not something you play with. It means business – it is deadly serious.

If you have ignored your feelings of anger for years, it won't take much to push you over the edge. Anger becomes unmanageable when it has been constantly ignored. It will change your usually pleasant and placid demeanour into one of rage – the result of years of pretending you are okay, that you shouldn't feel that way, that anger is not part of your life. Anger is part of everyone's life. It is an inbuilt safety valve.

Anger wants your acknowledgement – it wants your attention. It works hard for you. It wants you to recognise how important its contribution is to your life. It needs you to understand when your boundaries have been crossed or when your frustration has reached its maximum capacity; when it feels you have been disrespected by the outside world. It is on your side, alerting you to how you are feeling.

Anger wants the best for you. It's sick and tired of making excuses for people's behaviour or any unfair expectations placed upon you. It wants you to feel respected.

Take note and pay attention when you begin to feel your anger has been aroused. It's there to warn you that you are being pushed towards your limit!

Acknowledging your anger

So, what do you do with this feeling? Firstly, take some nice, deep, slow abdominal breaths. Sit with the feeling and acknowledge how angry you are. Your anger wants your acknowledgement, it wants you to be aware and to realise you have boundaries. You are not a robot – you are a human being with limits! Everyone has limits. Anger can terrify some people, so *find some private space for your personal work*. Fume! Acknowledging your anger does not hurt anyone – in fact, it simmers the situation down.

It might help to acknowledge your anger out loud. Say or better still *shout* how angry you are – you don't deserve this! Your acknowledgement is acting as a pressure valve that is beginning to let off steam. Affirm with your raised voice, 'I am so angry! I want more respect than this!' Admit to how you are really feeling. Vent, vent, vent. Acknowledge all that pent-up fury, hostility, self-righteous indignation, exasperation, frustration. Allow it to lose some of its high energy and intensity. It's good for you! The more space and acknowledgement you give to anger, the more in control and calm you will feel. Are you beginning to feel better? It's great to let those angry feelings out!

Your mission is to cut the power of anger the moment you recognise its warning signs. As with fear, acknowledgement is a significant pacifier.

I wasn't allowed to feel angry when I was a child, nor was I allowed to express it. It was forbidden in my family. People are scared of its power and don't know how to respond or what to do with it, so they choose to ignore it. You now know that it won't be ignored … forever.

Owning and acknowledging your anger, no matter what you are calling it, will remove its power over you. Feel proud of yourself – it's a very liberating and empowering thing to do, and you are saving yourself a lot of wear and tear, opting for a softer world that benefits you and everyone. It is another example of your personal power in action. Anger has a place in your life. It can also be very motivating when used positively.

Chapter 20

Fear of rejection vs emotional independence

How you treat yourself and others and how you allow others to treat you all originate from how you feel about yourself. Self-acceptance will ensure you set a higher standard for yourself.

Living a life of emotional independence creates an aura of confidence and peace. People will feel your presence and respond to you in new and powerful ways. There is something different about you, something special. They will be drawn to your attraction, sensing your essence; your inner strength; your willingness to live life on your own terms. Self-acceptance allows you to care for yourself and others in much more giving and sensitive ways, too.

Your old childhood fears are now sensing their place and becoming subservient to your progress. Fear of rejection, however, may take a little while longer to overcome. With every stride forward, rejection is part of the deal and the possible outcome. If you've ever been on an internet dating site, you'll know what rejection feels like and you may have experienced it many times! It still offends your ego. Today, feelings of self-acceptance and self-respect can move you beyond your ego and fear responses. You do not allow the fear of rejection to hinder your ongoing advancement or whether you and your ideas will be accepted. Each rejection is, in fact, making you stronger for the next.

Those sentiments also apply to the possibility of embarrassment or humiliation as you push through old boundaries. Remember, those feelings come from a time and place where you felt powerless and hadn't intellectually worked out that you were okay with or without others' approval of you.

Before I venture further, I would like to relate a poignant example of how the need to belong created severe, fear-based reactions for almost all my clients when I ran a classic glamour services business. The business was centred around makeup techniques, hairstyling to suit the individual's face shape, and colours that suited skin tones from seasonal colour swatches.

After I had shown each client how they could transform their appearance step by step … almost invariably they couldn't believe that they could look so beautiful! After staring at themselves for a minute or so, again, almost invariably, they would say: 'I can't look like this!' They would mention that their husband likes them to look 'natural', or their friends or family wouldn't like them looking like this. It was fear-based and too confronting!

Understand this: fear of offending the VIPs in our life is a potent killer of free will.

My clients were choosing to live beneath their enhanced beauty and potential for fear of upsetting someone important in their lives, perhaps fearing rejection or not feeling they were worthy or deserving of looking so beautiful.

So, fear of rejection, offending a VIP in our family or our generational need for acceptance is often more difficult to overcome than our need to make our own choices and forge our own path.

It's quite amazing how emotional dependence on the need to belong can be seen in this simple example, isn't it? Those choices are exactly what I am referring to all the way through this book — it is *that* powerful need to belong, subconscious childhood model emotional barricades patrolled by fear and our teenage need for generational acceptance, that keep us stuck in life processes and 'the system'. It is as simple as it is complicated.

When I was working in my glamour business, I was also gathering information about life processes for my personal understanding. I was not conscious of the childhood model or its fear-based overtures at that stage. It's fascinating, isn't it?

★★★

May I say, my books are never about creating problems for the individual or 'the group'. I am simply shining powerful light on the reasons why we have such difficulty exerting our free will. I do care about what people think of me, of course, but I won't allow an individual, 'the group' and their basic, fear-based conformity, tribal opinions, or generational philosophies to be my decision-makers. I accept total responsibility for myself and my behaviours and enjoy the privilege. I hope that makes sense to you.

Chapter 21

Your emotional relationship with yourself

When you recognise the many controls and tranquilising beliefs you brought with you from the past, you have an opportunity to override them with an intellectual response. Adjusting your self-image will help you to transform your life.

The relationship you have with yourself is extremely important. It sets the standard for all areas in your life. A strong, positive emotional relationship with yourself is one of the building blocks that helps you create your personal success. It leads directly to your personal power, deciding how far you will push the boundaries, how much effort are willing to put into yourself and how much you are prepared to take from others. Yes, it's another big one!

When you were a child, it was easy to see how you were feeling by your behaviour. Your behaviour was an extension of your feelings. Today, like a child, your feelings about yourself are transparent and on display, too. You are overtly telling the world how you feel about yourself.

Simply, what you are saying is:

- 'I'm not ready to be out there yet – that's why I'm staying out of the spotlight', or
- 'I don't know how to control my feelings – that's why I'm behaving so badly!', or
- 'Yes, I truly like myself – that's why I'm proactive'.

All these behaviours are true indications of the emotional relationship you are having with yourself at that moment.

You are creating a new world of emotional independence and emotional maturity, becoming conscious of just how powerful you *really* are when you see yourself as a separate, emotionally independent entity.

The power of emotional responsibility

Let's explore a few benefits of building a strong emotional relationship with yourself.

Creating your courageous self-image

Creating your courageous self-image was covered in Chapter 4, including creating a list of your own 'image builders'. You may like to revisit this Chapter now or wait until we review your self-image again in the last Section.

Overriding your need to belong

Today, new intellectual understanding allows you to position your emotional expansion above the need to belong and generational acceptance.

Emotional progress

Self-acceptance – that is, acknowledgement of your individuality – will lead naturally towards your emotional independence. Eventually, you will become less and less concerned about what others may think of you or about you – or even whether they think about you at all. Freedom!

Emotional nourishment

Your emotional base is your springboard to all that is waiting for you. It is your emotional life that provides the nourishment and satisfaction in your life. Without it you will live your life by rote: empty and joyless. You will go through the motions without ever feeling the joie de vivre. Knowing what brings joy into your life is what it's about, surely. Maybe you call it your passion. No matter what you call it, it is your responsibility to discover what gives you the feeling of emotional nourishment and satisfaction and do it as often as you can. It also has the benefit of locking you out of your resentment zone.

Your inner-world freedom

No-one can promise you more than you can give to yourself. When you stop looking outside yourself, you will find your answers within. Outside has nothing to offer – if it did, it would have already. True liking of yourself comes with no strings to the outside world. Freedom always begins in your inner world.

Keeping your promises

Keeping your promises, especially those you make to yourself, has the benefit of giving you even greater feelings of self-worth and self-respect. This is the beginning of a new trust and a new belief in yourself. It's more fuel for your personal power.

Making peace with your inhibition and self-consciousness

No-one is perfect – we all know that. But, deep down, you may be concerned about making a fool of yourself if you stand up to say something and make a mess of it. As a child, you would rather step back than risk embarrassment, rejection or feelings of foolishness. If you are still living in your inner child's world, you may think, 'OMG, I would rather die than risk XYZ!' But think about it this way: it seems like you die a little every time you choose not to speak up on matters important to you, mess or no mess, doesn't it? Operating from an intellectual basis and adopting the practices we'll discuss in Chapter 45: Self-talk will help you overcome this obstacle to personal power and free will.

Staying in tune with your feelings

Staying tuned in to yourself – knowing what you are feeling – is the beginning of a new world. Chapter 18 took you through the process. Keep working with your feelings. They are your power base. When you acknowledge and align with your feelings, you are in control – not *being* controlled.

The breakthrough: liking yourself

Liking yourself is a shift upwards in your emotional strength. It is a breakthrough, and the most necessary component of your personal and emotional development. Without it, you allow others to be more important than you, never realising your phenomenal personal power.

Liking yourself is replacing your inner child's insecurities with a new sense that you are okay. In fact, you are better than okay – you are flourishing with your evolving inner strength – feeling more peaceful, taking the high road with a 'can-do' attitude, affecting everything you are, everything you do and everyone you meet. You are beginning to align with the idea of expanding horizons, once obscured by clouds of self-doubt and uncertainty.

Personal power

Personal power goes hand in hand with your emotional independence. It is a feeling of being able to trust and believe in yourself, knowing you can handle whatever comes your way. It is your adult's sense of security. It is inner freedom. You have found a magical formula to work with your life and your spirit, while also creating a new sense of peace and dignity. Feelings of personal power are seductive. There is no greater motivator to the human spirit.

Emotional independence is the very essence of your soul. You are venturing into *uncommon* freedom. We will explore your emotional relationship with others in Section IX: Lightening your emotional load.

Chapter 22
Claiming your adult power

Relax – it's okay not to be liked.
In fact, it's impossible to be liked by everyone!

You did everything you could to be liked as a child – remember the people-pleasing and approval-seeking behaviours you engaged in? It's a natural tendency to want to be liked, but now it can hold you back.

Remember this: no matter what you do or who you are, you will always be judged – it is endemic in our society, in this world. People judge and criticise everything and everyone. We observed how to judge when we were judged as children. If those who are judging you are still living in their childhood model (and they probably are), those judgements will be based upon tribal and generational beliefs and conformity expectations – with a few 'supposed tos' thrown in for good measure.

Your judgers and criticisers have probably not reached your level of consciousness. You should expect to be judged and criticised when you step away from tribal and generational conformity. People's judgements and criticisms are always shaped by their belief systems – not yours.

As I wrote in an earlier chapter: generally, we cannot be emotionally independent and still fit into 'the group' and its culture, expectations and conformity issues. It's time to align with the spirit of your teenage self and recall how good it felt to go against 'the system'! The system works with conformity against personal power. It is now your personal power *overcoming* the system!

When you claim your adult power, it goes with the territory that you will need to override others' judgements and criticism. You are moving beyond crowd psychology. You are acknowledging your personal power and acting on your own behalf. It is your free will choosing to take precedence over belonging! Are you okay with that?

Basically, all you are doing is following through on your *adult* right to make your own choices. It is so basic when seen like this, isn't it? If you want your freedom, you need to overcome your fear of stepping away from others' conformity expectations – then, there is really nothing stopping you.

You are no longer the child taking orders – you are the adult making your own choices and using your personal power and free will to bring your choices into your life.

You are the only person in the world who can give your inner child the security and certainty it craves. You now know that the fear you feel when you attempt to push past old boundaries is your inner child's fear coming through your subconscious mind. Chapter 28: The dynamics of fear – an intellectual departure will give a full explanation of this process.

As I have said many times, fear is your greatest oppressor. Until you fully appreciate and understand its many levels of power and how it interferes with your life, fear becomes the permanent custodian of your emotional independence, your personal power and your free will.

Let me give you a perfect personal example of emotional contraction. When I was 20 years younger than I am today and hadn't yet discovered the childhood model, I bought an older inner-city apartment with fabulous views for one of my professional real estate projects. As it hadn't been modernised, it needed me to perform miracles. I loved decorating older homes and apartments with great bones that leaned towards wonderful transformations. I had pulled up the carpet, had an electrician remove all the old lighting, pulled down the old curtains, pulled up the rest of the chipped and missing floorboards, removed old wallpaper. The kitchen needed to be replaced so all the old cupboards and appliances had to go, too.

For reasons of space and economy, I decided to leave the old kitchen foundations in place and build around them with 'classic modern' new materials and benchtops. I chose the paint colours and textures; the light fittings; the parquetry flooring in the entrance, kitchen and dining area. The roman blinds were measured and ordered, and the work began.

I wanted something completely different for the kitchen wall tiles, preferring not to use the latest idea of glass splashbacks. In my search, I came across oblong gold tiles which fitted perfectly between the benchtop and the overhead cupboards in the neutral-coloured kitchen, with beautiful parquetry flooring extending into the dining area.

The builder I had been employing to replace the kitchen cupboard doors and benchtops mentioned that he was consummate at cutting and gluing tiles and that he could include installing the tiles for an additional hundred dollars or so. His work, up to that point, had been fine, so I agreed that he could do the job. I said to him, 'I will be back in the morning at 8 am. Please don't start the tiles until I arrive'.

Before I left that evening, I placed several of the tiles on the left side of the kitchen wall with the pattern facing right, which flowed naturally with our eye direction. Given that I was right-handed and that we always read from left to right, the tiles were perfectly positioned.

When I entered my apartment the next morning at the agreed time, I could smell glue! I walked through the loungeroom and into my kitchen and, to my horror, the builder had not only glued the gorgeous patterned high-gloss oblong gold tiles from right to left, but they had all been glued onto the wall with the pattern going the wrong way. Further, the tiles at each end of the wall that he had cut to fit had been chipped during the process but had been glued onto the wall anyway!

I couldn't believe my eyes! I said, 'Oh no, they are all going the wrong way! They should go from left to right with the pattern going the same way – the way I had the tiles standing. Can you please take them down?' He said, 'Oh, that won't be possible; they're already "going off"!'

Every time I walked into my kitchen from that day forward, I regretted not insisting he remove the tiles, whether they were 'going off' or not. In retrospect, I should have been the one 'going off'! It took the gloss off my beautiful new kitchen. *I let him get away with it because I was still living in my childhood model's comfort zones and emotional constriction.* I learnt a valuable lesson that day. (By the way, I later noticed he was left-handed!)

Can you recall a similar situation or lesson you have learned?

This is about clarifying your responsibility to yourself. Most of us don't set out to make our own lives difficult – other people make our lives difficult when they override our requests or step over our boundaries and the line of fair play.

Now, it's up to you to recognise when you are feeling disrespected: step into your adult power and use your free will to move beyond fear, intimidation and conformity issues.

Let's move forward and have some fun with the chain gang!

Section V: My challenges

Section VI
The chain gang

Overview		133
Chapter 23	The Establishment – who are they?	135
Chapter 24	Living within 'their' boundaries	140
Chapter 25	Unlocking your power	143
Chapter 26	Living up to your potential	145
Chapter 27	Setting conscious boundaries	150

Overview

Firstly, it is important that you understand I am *not* anti-establishment. In fact, I am very much in favour of the Establishment setting the ground rules and the standards for how we can live our lives, with a sense of security and the welfare of others in mind – if we choose.

Of course, it is not that simple. The trouble is, there is usually no possibility of a democratic outcome when dealing with the Establishment, who we shall meet in the next Chapter. It must always be 'their way'. They don't like to be questioned or challenged and they certainly don't like change – they are completely set in their ways. I have used the metaphor 'chain gang' to describe the inmates of this regime. My interpretation of a chain gang is a group of prisoners chained together working in monotony and repetition under the close supervision of the guards, fearful of making an independent move or making their own decisions. *The philosophy of the Establishment will always be 'one rule fits all'.*

Belonging is a basic need that we are now familiar with, but it is a double-edged sword. As an adult today, a single entity with a fully developed brain, you can assess whether conforming to the rules is still right for you or whether you would like to make your own arrangements. Again, may I say, there is nothing wrong with belonging per se; but it does have a downside, with many constrictive layers including fear and the group's psychology, which need to be overcome as you search for a much bigger life.

Know in advance that if you stand up and say what you need or want, as far as they are concerned you are causing them a problem. *They* won't change! Everything was fine till you stood up – you are creating the problem for them! See how it works? One on one or in a group situation, it's always the same. The defensive ones make it personal and begin to attack you. Their intractable mindset means they will never look at their role in the situation or negotiate with you.

You are expected by societal, tribal and generational philosophies to remain in the fear-based boundaries of conformity. There, there, good little child – you deserve a treat! Maybe now the maturing adult can decide for himself which treat he wants – how many and how often! ☺

We need to review and change the way we have been conditioned to think. Many believe that if a person goes against conformity, they create problems for the rest of us. In fact, the non-conformist is evolving – they are moving forward, leaving the rest of us behind!

Know that by stepping into your own power you are not breaking the law – you are breaking their rules. Those who complain about the non-conformists think that they are the law and what they stand for is the law – only in their conforming minds is that true. That's the distinction. You are perfectly entitled to live your life any way you choose – without their approval.

Later in this Section, a more sophisticated influence behind our hesitance to disarm those cords will be revealed. With this new insight, we can progress further. We will be looking into a variety of belonging cultures and their power and asking questions as we go forward.

Chapter 23
The Establishment – who are they?

We need to employ our imagination with this one,
allowing it to run free.
Knowing 'they' don't like to be questioned,
let's ask them tonnes of questions!
Let's challenge their self-appointed authority

We will begin our search with an old-fashioned term, 'the Establishment', as we try to find out what may be holding you back. What is the Establishment? Who are they?

- Are they old fogeys who sit in judgement, gavel in hand, and insist that everyone should live their lives in the past, using old perspectives?
- Are they younger, still living within the boundaries of their upbringing?
- Are they people who have never left the security of their comfort zones?
- Is their world serious and personal, like a child?

- Are they people who are stuck in their childhood model beliefs?
- Have they ever left the safety of their background?
- Do they believe life has limits – that possibilities are limited?
- Have they ever pushed the boundaries of their potential or possibilities?
- Is their world black-or-white, yes-or-no, can-or-can't, with no grey areas?
- Are their lives fear-based?
- Have they ever decided for themselves which is the right path for them?
- Do they see non-conformity as a threat to their prized and self-elevated position?
- Do they see dependence as normal?
- How do they see the meaning of 'individual'?
- Another clue: check the basics of the childhood model.

Do you have any questions for them? (Remember, they don't like to be questioned!)

_____
_____
_____
_____
_____

Now, let's have a look at a variety of words that could be used to describe the Establishment. You can then pinpoint exactly what the Establishment means to you, bringing you closer to your understanding. Do any of these resonate with you?

- control
- the master
- upper class
- force
- important
- rulers
- outrank
- society
- the hierarchy
- higher class
- the influence
- power
- superiority
- command position
- dominant
- recognised position
- authority
- absolute
- sovereignty
- the elders

Any others?

_____

_____

_____

_____

_____

The Establishment will always see themselves as your protector. Fear, in its many forms, dictates the philosophies of the Establishment. Do any of the following statements sound familiar?

- 'This is the way we do it.'
- 'This is the way it has always been done, and the way it will be done in the future.'
- 'We rule – it has always been that way and we know how it works!'
- 'This is the tried-and-true version of how you should live your life.'
- 'Don't give it another thought – we have the situation under control.'

- 'You don't have to worry about changes – there will be few, if any, on our watch.'
- 'You must *never* step across the line – we may not be able to rescue you. The other side will, no doubt, be thwarted by difficulties. Better the devil you know.'
- 'You must be loyal to your tribal family, your generation and all their rules – no matter what!'
- 'Remember this: every rule is for your benefit.'
- 'When you break the rules, you risk jeopardising your position among us.'
- 'We are the last word!'

Does it sound like a parent speaking to a child or a young adult? Can you think of any other statements they may use?

Where do we, today's adults, get the erroneous notion that we must continue to live as if we were still children? From our childhood model and adolescent years, fear, conformity issues, not wanting to be in the spotlight? Any others?

What does the Establishment offer the individual? There are benefits to living within their tight structures; this is where the maturing individual once again begins to feel stuck:

- The Establishment gives the participant a sense of security.
- The Establishment creates the image of solidarity and certainty.
- The Establishment can almost promise the individual there will be no change.
- The Establishment creates a sense of unity; united we stand, divided we fall.

Would you like to add to the above list?

_____

_____

_____

_____

_____

So, clearly, everything about the Establishment is about itself. They like to uphold this position to further empower themselves and continue to control and maintain 'the order' over us. This was perfectly sound reasoning when we were children, adolescents and teenagers – perhaps even young adults – but now, as maturing adults, we need to question such strictures and structures.

Note: you might be wondering if the Establishment ever changes their strict viewpoints. The consensus appears to be that yes, they do eventually – but only when there is enough momentum from within the group or when they fear a backlash from the general membership.

Chapter 24

Living within 'their' boundaries

Conformity is high on society's agenda to maintain discipline and order, but who says adults need to perpetuate their childhood conformity? Where did that rule come from?

Conformity means there is 'one rule that fits all'. We know, as adults, that can be a difficult fit. We are all so different. How is it possible to impose a single way of thinking over every adult's fully developed intellectual brain? This is another perfect example of how our childhood model's immediate subconscious responses override our ability to analyse such situations, when we are unaware.

Let's get the heavy stuff out into the open and take a closer look at how people may hold power over you.

Who makes you feel disempowered? How do you feel disempowered? When?

_____

_____

_____

What's the energy like between you and your oppressor?

What do you do with your frustration? Do you become angry with yourself?

Basically, controlling personalities use fear and rely upon your naivety and gentleness to work for them – against you. Fear and naivety become the bullies of the unconscious adult. Some of the fears you might be holding on to include:

- Fear of abandonment – this is a primal fear for every child in their childhood model
- Fear of embarrassing or humiliating yourself
- Fear of rejection
- Fear of losing your position within the family, community and so on
- Fear of not belonging
- Fear of being on your own
- Fear of demotion
- Fear of becoming an outcast
- Fear of not being able to survive if you step away from 'their' protection.

Any others?

___

Does the phrase 'this will hurt me more than it will hurt you' sound familiar to you? What other phrases does your oppressor use to control you?

___

Who else, besides the Establishment, intimidates you? What exactly are you intimidated by?

___

Okay, we now have a much broader appreciation as to why it has been so difficult to move away from the status quo. Now let's dig deeper.

Chapter 25

Unlocking your power

Nothing outside yourself can give you security. You build security into your life when you like, believe and trust in yourself, resulting in a willingness to become emotionally independent, using your personal power and your free will – no longer breaking rocks with the chain gang.

Now, I would like to upset the perspective we have drawn about the Establishment in the previous chapters and offer a surprising new twist.

What if I said: eventually, we become part of the Establishment. That is, we become an extension of our tribal families' and our generation's codes of conduct when we continue to uphold 'the order'. Continuing to live our lives emotionally conforming to fit in – just like the child in the model – over and above our own emotional independence results in us supporting 'them'! We make them more important than ourselves. *This is the base of your new understanding; your new life!*

We uphold the tradition of conformity and lack of change when we continue to live within 'their' fixed order and don't speak up or choose a different way – a bespoke way – to live our lives.

You may like to review the questions we asked of the Establishment in Chapter 23 and the questions I asked of you in Chapter 24. Check your answers to further understand how it all comes about and why we have been on autopilot. Simply stated, what we are realising is that all major conformity issues have been created by our inner child's need to belong and our teen's need for generational acceptance. The questions asked of you in Chapter 24 were necessary to provide you with an up-to-date version of where you are in your development regarding conformity issues.

Do you need to sit with this idea a little longer? What are you thinking/feeling?

_____

_____

_____

_____

_____

There is more of 'them' than 'us', because we didn't understand the powerlessness in the childhood model and its conformity pressures, or our teen's need for acceptance by its generation. Quite possibly, they don't, either. *I don't want to minimise this one*: it can be extremely difficult going against the crowd and its philosophies when we don't understand where our feelings of emotional intimidation are coming from. I want more than the Establishment has to offer and I like to choose for myself – how about you? I hope this is making sense to you.

Now, it's time to get among the more intricate, menacing, fear-based cords, closer 'to home', that keep you small and emotionally stunted.

Chapter 26
Living up to your potential

Let's reiterate: the Establishment is never about the individual or its freedom. It's about conformity and the group running the show — whoever that may be.

I have often wondered: does the Establishment ever step back and intellectualise their own position? Maybe it's more like an unconscious acceptance that this is the way it is, the way it's always been and the way it will always be. That the people who go against 'Centre Management' (my symbolic term) — who forge a life for themselves as individuals — are seen as the troublemakers, misfits, degenerates and rebels. Those who appear different make the majority feel uncomfortable. 'Centre Management' is then forced to tighten its ranks and make the free spirits among us into examples; this causes the majority to feel even more afraid to leave.

In Chapter 8 we analysed and severed (intellectually and maybe even psychically) the subconscious cords that have been preventing you from living a much bigger life — particularly a much bigger emotional life. But, for the sake of curiosity and clarity, let's take a look at why 'the centre' is such a difficult fit for some of us.

Do any of the following statements ring true?

- 'It feels unreasonable.'
- 'It feels stuck in a time warp.'
- 'I feel squashed.'
- 'I feel unimportant.'
- 'I feel my needs are not taken seriously, often disregarded.'
- 'I feel disrespected.'
- 'There's no room for expansion.'
- 'I feel I can't progress.'
- 'I feel generally unsupported when I try to step away.'
- 'I feel like I'll never be able to run my own life with all their rules.'
- 'I feel disempowered.'
- 'I'm an individual – how can one rule fit all?'

Are you tired of all their rules and their conforming expectations? Let me ask you this:

- Is it time to take over and manage your own life?
- Is it time to stand on your own and know what dignity feels like?
- Is it time to break away from conformity and everyday rules?
- Are you ready to make your own choices – live the way you dream it could be – not concerned about what the Establishment, or anyone else for that matter, may think?

It's time to liberate your spirit. Stepping away from the middle ground is where you must make your break. The middle ground doesn't move – if you want something different, you must be the mover and shaker of your life and go after what you want. Basically, you must move away from the centre to rejuvenate your spirit and feel alive!

I was always in trouble in my teens for wanting to be the decision-maker of my life. I needed so badly to decide what was right for me. My parents and other elders of the 'tribal family' were not happy with my reasoning or my behaviour and openly said so, but I needed to push the boundaries and find out what worked for me – potholes and all.

My marriage and later becoming a mum slowed me down. In fact, my spirit had almost flattened – or do I mean flatlined? I became someone else, someone I didn't particularly like – being held down by unwritten, constrictive philosophic rules and the ethos of the institutions of marriage and motherhood. My spirit had lost itself in the interpretation. My teen spirit was left wanting, waning, yearning. But, as they say in the classics, you can't keep a good girl down … forever! ☺

Defiance – Secrets of Your Midlife Crisis is about your adult choices and affirming the right to be yourself. It is about you taking the control of your life out of their hands. It's you who decides how you want to live your life, redefining who you are as an adult, no longer conforming as a child.

I need to make this clear: free will is your right – it is your right to live your own way, able to stretch your emotional wings and in the process rejuvenate your spirit, which has, most likely, taken second place most your life … until now.

Let's be clear about another point, too: it is those individuals who choose to move away from the centre who make revolutionary changes for our society. They should be applauded.

If they had stayed in the centre, we would be without the amazing artists, writers, architects, scientists and so on who contribute to and advance our society. It's so important that we acknowledge the right to forge our own paths, without worrying too much about the flack that will probably come down from those who prefer to stay within the status quo. It's all about adult choices.

I need you to understand: the Establishment will rarely change; it will uphold its own rules. You will be fighting those rules for the rest of your life – be aware of this. If you want more or something different to what is on offer, you must make it happen for yourself. You must step outside their fear-based boundaries and their rules and live your life away from centre.

Also realise: it's never about you. The people who oppose you and your progress are doing so because of their own beliefs. They are protecting themselves, their position and their need for certainty. They are security-conscious people with their egos and fear running the show with a scarcity mentality. They are scared of you – because you are different, and because you are willing to push old fear-based boundaries. By doing so, you are disrupting and disturbing their sense of power and security.

One more thing: it's never *personal*; they treat everyone who throws a shadow over their self-proclaimed reigning rights as a potential threat or obstacle. Do not think, for one moment, that you are being singled out. The same treatment would be given to anyone who threatens their authority or opposes them and their 'higher position' in some way.

When you realise it can never be what you want it to be, you need to let go – even if you don't want to move away from the pack. This is an adult's choice. If you continue fighting, trying to get them to see your point of view, you will only hurt yourself and, quite possibly, your health will eventually suffer.

I write with authenticity because I have experienced everything I write about in my books. My journey has been a '*mind*field' and an emotional eye-opener. Over the years I have experienced frustration, lack of support and general disrespect and discouragement, as well as deja vu reminders of my teenage feelings (not being heard or taken seriously) – not good for the human spirit! When I finally realised it was *always* going to be 'their way', I withdrew – no longer willing to bang my head against a brick wall.

There is a conscious art to knowing how far you can push the boundaries with a person or an institution that is on a different frequency and life path to you, without hurting yourself and compromising your health.

The good news: when you get to this level in your understanding, you will suddenly realise you don't need to ask for permission or their approval. It really is that simple. It means you are free to walk your own path any time you make that decision. You are taking the initiative and deciding the best way to live your life. It's the only reasonable and smart conclusion for anyone trying to expand their possibilities beyond traditional conformity.

Remember, the first time is always the hardest – after that, you will feed on the rejuvenation of your spirit and want to repeat those feelings.

Chapter 27
Setting conscious boundaries

> *We are striving to create a more conscious understanding between living within tribal and generational conformity and their structures, and the predictable developing needs of the adult who is trying to expand and satisfy his maturing interior and exterior life.*

As you move closer towards your freedom, you will be:

- seeking cooperation and reconciliation between old dictates and your current needs
- transitioning a black-or-white, either/or world into shades of grey
- transcending fear-based comfort zones to expand and progress your life
- transforming emotional dependence and conformity to emotional *in*dependence and free will to progress your adult's rite of passage.

You are redefining and expanding the boundaries found in your childhood model and asserting authority over your teen's need to remain within its peer group acceptance philosophies.

You are taking adult responsibility for yourself and giving yourself the authority that is commensurate with that responsibility.

Responsibility without authority is a losing proposition. You, as an adult, can deliver both to the table.

There is no blame, no victim mentality, no restrictions or limits – it is you giving yourself permission to take responsibility for your life without deferring to the emotionally limiting boundaries that are present in conformity issues in the previous two stages of your development. It is your hard-earned, united, emotional *in*dependence and intellectual free will in action; exquisite free will. *'Hello Mustang!'* More later.

Power struggles are common in relationships where boundaries were not set in the early stages. It's extremely difficult to reclaim your power once you have handed it over. People will always push boundaries in *their* favour.

Setting boundaries is a difficult proposition for most of us. We learnt to be 'agreeable' as children to fit in and we want acceptance by our generation as well.

We need to overcome our fear of upsetting people and realise that setting boundaries is our adult responsibility to ourselves.

You don't need to justify your position, but you could say, 'I value this relationship and to avoid any possibility of complications in the future, I would like to set some boundaries now'. The trick is to know *your* boundaries.

Becoming adept at handling people will help you in all walks of life. There are adult education courses that will help you deal with 'difficult' people; I have done my fair share over the years and recommend them. Books are also a valuable source. It comes down to transcending your fear of standing up to whoever they may be and being willing to say what is troubling you in your relationship with them — softly and gently. It also means expecting a positive change or you will be prepared to let go of the relationship. Compromising your self-worth and dignity will never raise the bar. The people in your life today may not be in your life in five years. Your best friend will always be you.

Section VI: My challenges

Section VII

More reasons for not owning your free will

Overview		157
Chapter 28	The dynamics of fear – an intellectual departure	159
Chapter 29	Know your seducers	169
Chapter 30	Liberating groundless beliefs	175

Overview

Remember: fear was built into our DNA in primitive times. It was put there to keep us safe when we lived in a hostile environment with a much shorter lifespan. Nothing has changed – it still wants to keep you safe today. It wants to protect you. When seen in this light, fear is on your side.

Today, you are working towards claiming a much bigger life – a life of your own, implementing strong, rational ideas and concepts to progress your adult position. However, because you are stepping away from your fear-based comfort zones, have no doubt, fear will be present.

Fear needs to be understood and *overcome*, otherwise it will continue managing your life ad infinitum.

Keep this in mind: you are a force, too, when you understand fear and persist anyway!

We will bring awareness of your seducers into the light and then we'll liberate old groundless beliefs.

But first, let's check out some new ways to deal with fear.

Chapter 28
The dynamics of fear – an intellectual departure

Fear is life's greatest oppressor.
When we allow fear to bully us and manage our lives,
we 'settle', never reaching our potential.

Fear is part of our survival DNA. It goes back to primitive times, when it warned us of imminent physical danger – when we didn't have time to think about a reaction. Our adrenals reacted with a 'fight or flight' response by pumping adrenaline into our system, increasing our heart rate, boosting energy levels and elevating our blood pressure – making us stronger and faster. When used for this purpose, it is an extremely good warning system.

The fear you felt as a child, which kept you safe and in line, is the same fear you feel today. But without an intellectual response, it is now separating you from a much bigger and more satisfying life. To advance, you need to understand the tactics and manoeuvres fear uses to control you.

Fear is by far your most potent disciplinarian. Unfortunately, when you allow fear to conduct your life, the outcome often means settling for a 'this is it' kind of life.

When you settle:

- you take a defeatist position – effectively, you give in or give up
- you suspend your potential
- you remain emotionally small and contracted, squashing any feelings of personal power
- it leads straight into your resentment zone.

Any others?

_____

_____

_____

Settling is a major contributor to feelings of bitterness and anger towards yourself, others and life generally. It adds to the chip on your shoulder.

I discovered that a resistance to change – or, indeed, trying anything new – is usually based upon perceived fears of the 'what if' variety. Those fears eventually translated into my avoidance behaviours. Is this making sense?

Now, your intellect, emotional *in*dependence and new beliefs about yourself – keyed into liking who you are today – are formidable opponents, too. Have no doubt: you are more than equal to fear, childhood self-doubts and all of life's challenges. But without intellectual understanding, fear remains the permanent custodian of your personal power and free will.

We will take a deeper look at fear shortly, but first I would like to draw your attention to the way your body interprets your everyday stressors as fear and the subject of adrenal fatigue. This is my simple version. Again, awareness is powerful.

Adrenal fatigue or 'modern day burnout' is slowly becoming a recognised medical syndrome. Your two tiny adrenal glands are located on top of each of your kidneys. They supply your body with adrenaline, among other things. It is part of your parasympathetic nervous system. When you are feeling chronically stressed (tired and wired), adrenaline sympathetically enters your system. Those reserves, once used to prepare your body for physical danger, are now being set off by everyday stressors. Adrenaline is becoming your daily dose of normal.

In other words, primitive 'fight or flight' responses are being activated by modern-day lifestyles. Your body is not able to distinguish between physical fear and stress-related issues. When you feel under pressure for long periods of time, you presume your state of nervousness and uneasiness is normal.

The problem arises when your parasympathetic nervous system is not given enough rest and recovery time to build its precious reserves of adrenaline, resulting in an imbalance between the two nervous systems. When you are suffering from adrenal fatigue, a complete change in attitude and lifestyle is often the only long-term answer. Fear, with its associated stressors, seems to be an ongoing source of frustration, doesn't it?

In other words, reviewing the way you deal with the stressors in your everyday life will enable you to live within those primitive, physical confines and remain healthy, strong and energetic.

From this perspective, it is crucial to find out what is causing such high adrenaline demands, and what you can do to reduce your stress levels. Should you wish to investigate adrenal fatigue further, there are some excellent books available on this subject.

Let's check some of the physical symptoms of fear that may be a daily constant in your life *without* any real physical danger. Do any of these feel familiar?

- uneasiness
- pounding heart
- tightness in your chest
- short, shallow breathing
- feeling light-headed or dizzy
- hyperventilating
- constriction/lump in your throat
- sleep problems
- jumpy nervous system
- increased pulse rate
- increased blood pressure
- dilated pupils
- muscles tense and energised
- listlessness
- excessive perspiration
- nausea
- neck and shoulder tightness
- heart palpitations
- dry mouth
- restlessness
- apprehension
- confusion
- panic or anxiety
- irritability
- agitation
- sweaty palms

Any others?

_____
_____
_____

Where, in your physical self, do you feel fear? In your stomach, solar plexus or somewhere else?

_____
_____
_____

Fear likes to play games with you, as it did when you were a child: concealing its identity, camouflaging itself as something else, keeping you safe.

I lived with what I believed to be low-grade anxiety most of my life; but, in fact, it was fear! And, as it turned out, most of my fears were perceived fears and most were related to the fears in my childhood model. Of course! Those anxieties were passed directly onto me, through my subconscious mind, when I encountered similar anxiety-producing situations.

Without an intellectual response to fear, anxiousness becomes a way of life when we feel helpless and powerless. Ah-ha!

It's helpful to know how fear sneaks up on you and into your life. Perhaps fear has convinced you, too, that what you are feeling is not fear; perhaps you think of it as anxiety or a sense of uneasiness, nervous tension or stress. Sometimes fear can appear as aggression, confusion or feelings of intimidation. Procrastination, indecision, avoidance and self-doubt may also be a consequence of fear. Whatever it is, your 'fight or flight' responses perceive it to be a danger or threat to your physical self, impacting your precious adrenaline reserves.

Here are some examples of a fear response today *without any physical threat* being present:

- fear of ridicule
- fear of humiliation
- fear of consequences
- fear of embarrassment
- fear of standing alone
- fear of rejection

- fear of success
- fear of failure
- fear of the unknown.

Because fear often disguises itself as something else, you need to understand its tactics and the character it presents to you. What are your tell-tale signs that fear is present? Are they the same signs each time or do they change depending on the circumstances?

_____

_____

_____

Is your sense of fear related to physical danger, or your current emotionally stressful situation? Are you expanding your comfort zones? Does fear present as intimidation? Do you lose interest or avoid if you feel intimidated?

_____

_____

_____

You are taking charge of the game when you are intellectually and intuitively becoming aware of your fear's tactics and covert strategies, conscious of some of its fundamentals. Be aware also that every feeling you have is pre-empted by a thought! What were you thinking *immediately before* you became aware that fear had entered your life?

_____

_____

_____

Is it a perceived fear or an actual fear?

What causes stress or anxiety in your life?

Is there anything you avoid so that you feel less stressed?

If aggression is part of your fear response, what presses your buttons?

Does indecision or procrastination result in anxiety or confusion for you? Like me, are you then likely to make a quick decision to eliminate this feeling? Is it one of your patterns?

What types of situations cause you to worry or feel overwhelmed, nervous or intimidated?

_____
_____
_____

Is there anything in your life you fear facing? Please list your reasons, too.

_____
_____
_____

Do you remember any examples of how or where your fears originated?

_____
_____
_____

Can you think of any examples of situations where fear has impacted your progress?

_____
_____
_____

I discovered that when you are expecting a certain outcome, but suddenly you get something different, fear appears. As I mentioned in an earlier Chapter, surprise is fear's ally. It really is a menace, isn't it? The more you understand your oppressor, the greater the probability you have of *overcoming* its stranglehold. Your adrenals will thank you, too. You can use the above kind of questioning whenever fear is hindering your progress or if fear is the reason you may not be enjoying your life to the fullest.

Remember: you are a formidable opponent too – when you are conscious!

How is it possible to manage fear and self-doubt to progress your emotional development?

Here are a few techniques:

- Become conscious of and understand the strategies and tricks fear uses to control you.
- Breathe. Deep abdominal breathing keeps the mind calm and the body strong.
- Acknowledge your fear – this will reduce its severity. Simply saying, 'I feel my fear, but I need to expand my life; we can do this' provides a wonderful sense of free will and determination. You may have to acknowledge fear several times as you progress, but its severity will weaken each time you acknowledge its presence.
- Use affirming, positive self-talk; it is a wonderful fear and self-doubt diffuser. (Chapter 45 will expose the magic of this valuable tool.) My favourite affirmation when I feel fear: 'I am bigger than this situation – we can do this!'
- Practise yoga. I have found several simple and easy yoga positions can help to relieve stress.
- See fear for what it is: a barrier between you and a life of emotional independence, personal power and free will.

When you understand that fear is one of the major obstacles in your personal development, you can progress into the future with fear accompanying you (as it should), but not bullying you into submission. Great progress!

Now, with your new insights into fear, you can more easily identify and pacify your fears with acknowledgement, a new perspective and adult intellectual responses, saving a lot of wear and tear on your adrenals. Fear is no longer such a huge obstacle to your progress. You are now fully equipped to evaluate and handle fear and your current situation intellectually.

Let your frightened inner child know that fear can't hurt it, that you are taking charge of fear and taking the next step, shielding your inner child, and creating a much bigger future together.

Having said all that – challenging yourself to do things you are afraid of can be fun, and the rejuvenation of your spirit exhilarating. To feel alive, you sometimes need to do something that is hugely challenging for you – maybe something you thought you could never do. It's great for your sense of empowerment and supporting your 'can-do' attitude, too. It is your emotional freedom beckoning you to extend your boundaries and expand your horizons, giving you new opportunities and taking you to the next level.

Chapter 29

Know your seducers

*What seduces you? They are your
blind spots; your weak spots.*

Seducers, real or imagined, all have power over you. They are your inner soft spots – your heart over your head. It's important to know what they are because they translate into your vulnerability in the outside world. It's not nice when you feel used by others who will take advantage of your good nature and naivety. Learn about and stay aware of your seducers.

Is there anything you believe you can't live without? Can you name it/them?

_____

_____

_____

Must you be partnered? Do you find it difficult to be on your own?

_____

_____

_____

Do you need attention, recognition, compliments, kudos, appreciation or notoriety to feel okay?

_____
_____

Do you need to be popular?

_____
_____

Do you need to belong, need to be accepted, need to fit in?

_____
_____

Are you seduced by charm?

_____
_____

Are you a romantic?

_____
_____

Do you always have to be the nice guy?

_____
_____

Are material things your seducers? Fast or expensive cars, biggest house, best boat?

_____
_____

Any others? (Remember, admitting to your vulnerabilities will reduce their power over you.)

___

Let's investigate some of the main ways seducers can rob you of your power.

Naivety

Do you get caught up in idealism? Do you think everyone has the same ideals as you? Do you believe no-one could ever be corrupt or hurtful in real life – only in the movies? Do you like to think that everyone is like you and has your principles?

___

A soft heart

A soft heart can be easily seduced. Do you always feel sorry for someone in a sad story or tough situation? See it for what it is – your seducer! Can you give any past examples?

___

Money

Ladies and gentlemen! Please don't give your money away – to anyone, especially to lovers, or any business proposition that sounds too good to be true.

Money is a form of power. It's part of your power. Money makes you more attractive. Money makes you strong and independent.

Know your seducers. Your vulnerability is at stake. Step back. Please don't allow your heart to rule your head. Never feel guilty, selfish or ashamed when you are not willing to 'donate' to someone's cause. You will have no regrets. What makes you vulnerable?

I'll say it again: you are so much more attractive when you have money. Stay alert.

Trust

If you are a trusting person, don't presume everyone else is. There are a lot of liars, cheats and manipulators out there – be careful, especially when your heart and your financial security are at stake. Ask yourself, 'What am I basing my trust upon?'

Think about this:

People who trust can usually be trusted; people who don't trust generally cannot be trusted.

Makes sense, doesn't it?

Power

Who or what do you give your power to? Is it a childhood belief? What are your reasons?

Do you ever hand your power over to someone who you think is more attractive, stronger, smarter or better educated than you? May I ask: are you financially dependent on that person?

Deserving

This one is thrown in for good measure. What don't you deserve? Why? Who said so?

Blaming

Is blaming one of your seducers? It's easy to blame — it lets you off the hook and you don't have to take any responsibility for your part in the scenario. Blaming further separates you from any feelings of personal power. There are no lessons learnt when you blame.

When are you likely to blame? Why?

How do you feel about yourself when you blame?

_____
_____
_____

Victim mentality

Feeling powerless, helpless and blaming everyone or one person for all your problems will never solve anything. It's another day, month, year or even decade wasted! No lessons have been learnt. A victim mentality makes you feel sorry for yourself.

Is fear playing a role in your victim mentality? Is there anything that scares you about taking responsibility for yourself?

No more violins! We are swapping violins for heavy metal bass guitars! ☺

Remember: there is no responsibility towards yourself in your childhood model. Today, when you transcend victim mentality, you will be free to take responsibility for yourself in all scenarios. You will feel your personal power when you stand side-by-side with your inner strength, assuring your inner child that you have this situation surrounded. You won't believe how powerful that action makes you feel. 'I am' is manifesting itself! There is nothing you can't handle today!

Jealousy

Is jealousy a seducer of your personal power and free will? It is covered in the next chapter.

Chapter 30
Liberating groundless beliefs

Knowing your seducers and challenging fear-based beliefs puts you in a powerful position. Let's liberate more.

Firstly, we'll begin with concerns about what other people may be thinking about you. Most of us seem to be concerned about this – *of course*. This kind of thinking began with our need to belong to secure our survival and our teen's need for acceptance by its generation. They are both natural, learnt and accepted positions. So, fearing repercussions if you step away from learnt positions and decide for yourself makes perfect sense, too, doesn't it?

You may be surprised to learn how infrequently people think about other people. Most of the time, they are totally consumed with themselves and their own problems. So, relax.

Let's begin by looking at some of the groundless beliefs you might be carrying that will hinder your progress.

Praise will change you into a brat

I was brought up in an era when praise was not given readily, if at all. (One might become a spoilt brat; or, worse, one might forget one's station in life – heaven forbid!) These days, I give myself lots of praise – it feels great, and it has a lovely softening effect on my physical and emotional wellbeing. You are worthy of praise, too. Give yourself plenty of superlatives regularly and wholeheartedly.

Relationships last forever

Staying where you are or refusing to move forward for reasons of security or to avoid upsetting anyone is not a long-term answer or in anyone's interests. Sometimes you need to leave relationships when you have outgrown them – for example, if you have nothing in common anymore or when your 'frequencies' no longer match. It is not personal; it is the way life works. It's about staying in tune, current with your stages of development and being aware of what is happening in your life. We all move forward at different frequencies. Enjoy each other's company when you are together and on the same frequency.

I have no power

Early in our personal relationships, we may be tempted and far too eager to go along with everyone and everything, not realising we have any power (usually to please – as we did as children). Trust me: it is extremely difficult, almost impossible, when you come to the maturing realisation that you do in fact have power, lots of power, then try to reclaim it later, especially after a long period of time. Always keep something for yourself – retain your sense of power. It is a great equaliser.

I can't have what they have

Let's explore the green-eyed monster. Here are some words to describe jealousy; circle or highlight the words that mean the most to you:

- resentment
- discontent
- distrust
- unworthiness
- contentious
- competitive
- bitterness
- hostile
- wish I could be you

- envy
- rivalry
- imitate
- undeserving
- possessiveness
- admire
- conflict
- anger
- self-doubt issues

Any others?

_____

_____

_____

Are you jealous of others' success? Material possessions? Partners?

_____

_____

_____

Where does the idea that you 'can't have what they have' originate from?

_____

_____

_____

If you want what they have, nothing is stopping you but groundless beliefs from childhood or your teen years. You are not powerless today: go after your dreams.

Rejection must be avoided

Rejection belongs to the fear family. Learn how to handle rejection – it won't hurt you! Remember, you are now working with the idea that you no longer need approval to feel okay about yourself. If you want a bigger life, rejection is part of the deal. Learning how to be on your own will also help you overcome feelings of needing acceptance to feel okay about yourself.

When you are 'out there' doing your own thing you must be prepared for criticism, judgements, ridicule and rejection. Your teen's need to be emotionally accepted by your generation is the current cord we are disarming to give you emotional independence from that group.

I'm not suggesting for a moment that it's easy. Heaven knows, becoming emotionally independent is one of the hardest things you will ever have to do to feel aligned with your power and freedom. That's why so few people do it! Liking yourself and self-approval will give you shelter on your journey into freedom.

Please believe it is okay not to be liked. Being liked by everyone is impossible anyway and being liked per se is not a prerequisite for happiness. Liking yourself today is your new benchmark!

I am dependent and powerless

Until we begin to question our beliefs and boundaries, we behave like fearful children, afraid that if we speak up or make our own decisions, we may be abandoned, rejected, criticised, ridiculed, embarrassed, judged, humiliated and so on. To a child, abandonment is terrorising! How will it survive? You can see clearly how all those issues began, can't you? That's not you today! I believe that most of our inner child's beliefs are the 'survival-based need to belong' variety, with a considerable number in the self-doubt category, too.

If you are still seeing yourself as a defenceless, helpless, powerless child who can't have what you want, then that is the way you will remain until you either become aware, want something badly enough or become passionate about something. You know how to work with fear now. When you become willing to transcend fear, you will evolve!

Is your glass half full or half empty?

How you think makes a big difference to what you are attracting into your life. Do you have an abundance or scarcity mentality? Is your glass half full or half empty?

_____

_____

If you are living with a scarcity mentality, everything you see and everything you want is in short supply: you will probably miss out, and you will have to work even harder to get what you want (if there is anything left for you). It is a very depressing way of living and viewing life. A scarcity mentality is fear-based and almost guarantees that you won't be able to have what you want – it can become a self-fulfilling prophecy. It's almost giving up or settling before you even try, isn't it?

When you work on overcoming (there's that word again) a scarcity mentality, you begin to see that life really does have abundance and myriad choices – there is a lot on offer 'out there'. Awareness of your learnt positions is more rejuvenation for your spirit.

Is there anything you could view differently to change your perspective?

_____
_____
_____

How will your changing position help you get what you want?

_____
_____
_____

Big picture – what is possible for you now?

_____
_____
_____

I don't deserve respect

How you treat or view yourself is a learnt behaviour. Do you treat yourself with respect?

_____
_____

Do you praise yourself for a job well done? How well you managed a difficult client? Compliment your appearance? Any others?

_____
_____

Do you appreciate and reflect on the amount of effort you have put into yourself to get to where you are today? If not, why not? What can you start with?

Do you give yourself time out to enjoy your life?

What makes you unique? Do you appreciate your differences? Why/why not?

Any others?

What other limiting beliefs do you have about yourself?

Can you track their origins?

Do any childhood limiting beliefs impact you today? How?

_____
_____
_____
_____
_____
_____

Make time to cultivate a new appreciation for yourself. It will help rejuvenate your spirit, too.

Section VII: My challenges

Section VIII

Creating a more 'lived-in' life

Overview		187
Chapter 31	Putting yourself first	189
Chapter 32	Disempowering 'personal'	191
Chapter 33	Choices	194
Chapter 34	What is stopping you?	196
Chapter 35	Confronting personal beliefs	202
Chapter 36	Building your powerful arsenal	208
Chapter 37	Character-building behaviours	212

Overview

Making smart choices that lean in your favour and advance your position is the adult's rite of passage. It is your prerogative, as an adult, to set your own standards and expectations and to live your life on your terms, with or without their approval.

Give yourself permission! No-one else's way will work for you. You know that, I know that. Your way, your terms, your path is the best way for you.

Ask yourself: 'how's my spirit?' Your answer will be a much closer gauge to your truth.

You, the adult – not your inner child or teenage self – are taking charge of your life and your future. The thoughts you are having now are determining the kind of future you are making for yourself. Time to liberate yourself further from old patterns.

In this Section, we will be searching for more ways to crack old, cemented barriers that create fear and anxiety when you lean against them, trying to create a much bigger life for yourself. You will also have a chance to nominate all your reasons for living a limited life as we proceed. It takes intestinal fortitude and determination to stand up to *your* old structures – no-one else's structures. You are using your exquisite free will to overcome your learnt way of dealing with life. Let's find out more.

Chapter 31
Putting yourself first

We all know that putting others first without allowing commensurate consideration for ourselves leads to anger and resentment issues – perhaps even regrets down the line.

One of the main aims of this book is to have you thinking like a delightful, *defiant adult brat!* I would love to inspire you to ask valid and progressive questions of yourself, such as:

- What's possible for me today?
- How do I *really* want to live my life?
- How do I see my future?
- What steps do I need to take to get there?

If you are a younger adult reader, you now have the supporting evidence that will allow you to live your life on your terms, to be here doing exactly what you need to do to connect with your higher self and your path towards your destiny. Those before you, like me, have not been quite so fortunate. My generation has often taken the position of 'others first'. We now know that does not work if we are to live without anger, resentments and regrets, and lingering feelings of bitterness. Each of us is, after all, a single entity.

My books are focused on reasons why we must put ourselves first, overcoming fear and emotionally dependent boundaries transcending our need to belong. 'Put your mask on first, then attend to others' is the modern way to live your life without anger, resentments and regrets stripping you of your dignity, power and the right to live your own life.

We will bring you closer to understanding yourself by asking such questions as:

- What makes you feel powerless?
- Who makes you feel powerless and why?
- How would you really like to live your life?

While we are still alive with reasonable health, it is never too late. So, if there is something you really want to do, you will find powerful reasons in this book to go ahead.

Let's test some of your conscious areas and give light to others.

Chapter 32

Disempowering 'personal'

*We have feelings, senses and intuition to guide us,
fear and anger to warn us. We are born self-protective.*

Your life is personal. My life is personal. Our childhood models were based upon personal. Remember, our inner child presumed that what it was learning was the only way – intellectually unable to reason that there were numerous ways with many different interpretations. To progress, the adult needs to let go of the childhood model's 'personal' interpretation, otherwise it creates problems for the adult that are not there. Personal is creating the problems. Personal is one-dimensional, too exacting, biased and limiting to work for the adult today. We need to expand our world, not to contract it further.

I believe that everything that comes into our lives begins as neutral. We make it something else when we put our skewed, personalised, unique interpretation on it, changing its original neutral character.

We need to disempower 'personal'.

Our personal life, experiences and unique interpretations are what we use to compare, filter or sort. They act as a base to help us understand our current circumstances or events, or to make sense of what we have just read, heard or observed. 'Personal' used in this context allows us the freedom to understand what is happening in the present or what we are reading, learning, etc. How could we make sense of what is happening in our lives now without our 'personal' perspective? Right?

However, once you have understood your 'personal' take on a situation or processed the meaning of what you have just read, heard or observed, you can then let go of your biased, 'personal' meaning and deal with it on a more generic, universal and impersonal level. This allows the adult wriggle room to conduct its life in a more mature, conciliatory manner, open to other interpretations and other ways of dealing with the same thing.

In other words, removing your 'personal' interpretation after it has given you an understanding of a situation and then seeing it in a neutral light enables you to expand your world instead of remaining in the tight, personal world of your childhood model with only one interpretation. This is where the grey areas make their mark on the maturing, reasoning, discriminating intellect, because it is now able to make such distinctions.

Personal and no alternative choices in the childhood model can now become generic, universal and impersonal meanings presenting multiple choices for the adult.

Does that make sense to you?

When you disempower personal, removing it from your transactions with others, you can see the big, generic picture and the situation more clearly with any number of choices – especially those that are even more beneficial for you. Effectively, you are creating a much bigger world for yourself.

I know this sounds contradictory to everything I have written previously, but seen in a wider context:

- it is and should be our drive for freedom that is personal and non-negotiable, but ...
- the way we conduct and manage our lives and relationships with others should be as malleable, conciliatory and flexible as possible – without compromising our position – to progress to a win-win.

Let me give you a personal example. I had lived a long time in my childhood model's either/or world, often feeling 'stuck' but thinking I had no alternative choices. One day, I watched someone close to me negotiate a most agreeable outcome for all concerned. I remember being quite shocked and wondered how and why that move didn't compromise our positions. It was the opposite to my childhood observations and my either/or understanding, and I was in conflict! Once I intellectually and logically reasoned that grey areas (i.e. negotiation) could, in fact, be agreeable for all parties including myself and that conciliatory action was life-enhancing, my world began to open exponentially. It was a big 'ah-ha' moment for me and one I have never forgotten.

Can you think of a personal example of a situation where you have opened your world by adopting a new and different understanding of your childhood model's interpretation?

_____

_____

_____

_____

I realise, of course, that this is a beautiful but idealistic way to live and that it will not always be possible to be conciliatory, as we have discussed throughout this book. However, choosing to live your maturing life powerfully and congruently is your new reality and it is your freedom to do so that is non-negotiable.

Chapter 33
Choices

Our lives can be summed up by the word 'choices'.

The aggregate 'you' is based upon all the choices made for you or that you have made for yourself to date. Our lives are based upon the choices we make every day, even though some may not seem like choices at the time. Liking who you are today practically guarantees that your choices will change and become biased towards you and your best interests. I do not mean selfishness – I am writing about the choices available to you that could make your life a joy. *Your* choices – not someone else's. You deserve your biased choices. Remember that!

We are all hardwired in our childhood. May I say, I did everything that was expected of me (in my childhood model), but ultimately, my life was still a mess; it didn't work out! Of course, it didn't work out – how could it? Living your life in the imagination and beliefs of a literal child means you will always take the subordinate position, feeling you are not free to make your own choices. That is, until you become intellectually involved with your life – where you are now.

As mentioned in Chapter 8, there is no self-responsibility in the childhood model. It was a black-or-white world – alternative choices were missing. We can only give ourselves the latitude to run our lives 100 per cent when we take total responsibility for our lives and the outcomes of all our choices. No-one else's rules – okay? They will never work for the conscious adult.

This means that there are no excuses; there's no avoiding, no blaming, no victim mentality, no 'he said, she said'. It's about you living your life without the need for such fallback positions … remember the heavy metal bass guitar?

It's time to ditch the backseat drivers and create a life that is truly independent. 'I am' is taking over.

Chapter 34

What is stopping you?

Overcoming is an ongoing and major theme throughout our lives – a major part of our life's work.

Expansion is a natural progression; without it, we would still be living in caves. Businesses expand, someone imagined the wheel; we have even invented ways to go to the moon. As mentioned previously, the Universe loves expansion – so when we are living within this natural, intentional, progressive phenomenon, humans *should* continue to push old boundaries – elevating their positions, too.

Now, let's check some areas that may be hampering your advancement. Bullet points for your answers will suffice as you bring more awareness into focus.

Avoidance or settling

Are you using avoidance or settling as a way of handling your adult life? Do you think that if you avoid a situation, the problem will go away? Can you name the benefits? (Seriously – there is always something.)

_____

_____

Never again

Do you make hard-and-fast rules about how you will or won't live your life by using such phrases as, 'never again' or 'I won't ever do that again'? We all say things like that, especially when we have been hurt.

Note: your subconscious mind is still taking orders from you, especially when those orders are backed up by a highly emotional state. Your subconscious mind operates without humour and is always serious. It will obey your instructions and commands, doing everything in its power to make it happen for you. Be careful what you say; be careful what you wish for!

Would you like to list your 'never agains' and why you said them, so you can clearly see how these types of statements have the power to reduce the size of your world by limiting your future choices?

Changes

Do you want 'what is' to be 'what was'? If you can accept that everything changes, you can begin to work with the flow of life and today's reality rather than fighting it. Fighting is compounding the situation into a no-win for you. Where do you feel stuck? Which areas are hardest for you to let go of?

Daydreaming

As a child, were you chastised for daydreaming? Give yourself permission. The modern term is 'visualising'. Develop your daydreams. What do you like to daydream about?

_____
_____
_____

Soul food

What feeds your soul? What do you absolutely love to do? Would it be possible to turn it into a business? What would you need to do to make this happen?

_____
_____
_____

Disempowerment

Do you feel powerless sometimes? This is a *big* question. What makes you feel powerless?

_____
_____
_____

When do you feel powerless?

_____
_____
_____

How do you feel powerless?

Who makes you feel powerless and why? What do they get out of bullying or intimidating you? (Don't worry about the idea that we allow people to make us feel powerless – this is about you becoming aware of your behaviour when you feel bullied or intimidated.)

On the flip side: what makes you feel empowered?

Now, what changes may be possible for you with your new insights?

Difficulties

Acknowledging and admitting what is difficult for you will reduce its power over you.

It's difficult for me to:

_____
_____
_____

What can you work on to reduce some of the weight of your difficulties?

_____
_____
_____

Embracing new possibilities

How would you *really* like to live your life? A different location? A different lifestyle?

_____
_____
_____

What needs to change for this to happen?

_____
_____
_____

Do you have a question or idea that needs time to develop? If so:

1. write out the question on a whiteboard or a sheet of paper
2. leave the question in clear view
3. focus on the question several times every day
4. write down your answers as they come through.

Slowly, over the next week or so, expect to see an amazing number and surprising diversity in your answers.

Chapter 35
Confronting personal beliefs

*What beliefs are you basing your life upon today?
Are they up-to-date and realistic?*

Old beliefs and their negative spin need to be sorted before you can create a sense of personal power. Beliefs become your self-fulfilling prophecies. We need strong, powerful beliefs that allow our free will to come into play. Challenge what you believe about yourself today and your potential.

Let's begin by asking some questions relating to you. What are your limits? What can't you have?

Your childhood model stores your limits. Maybe it was something you were told you couldn't have as a child or a teen before your intellectual brain was fully developed. There is nothing stopping you now. What do you think you can't have? Is it connected to jealousy?

Now you are aware, what do you need to do to make it possible for you today?

Disempowering beliefs

What is chipping away at your self-esteem? Be as definitive as possible. Do you feel you are not attractive enough? How? What can you do about it? Not enough education? Which course will help you to progress? Do you have any needs you are not fulfilling? How are they affecting you? What can you do about them?

Is there anything about yourself that can't be changed that you find difficult to accept, but perhaps could be seen from a different angle or in a softer light?

What beliefs do you have about yourself or life in general that are disempowering you?

What do you deserve?

What don't you deserve?

Do you believe you are unlovable? To prove this self-fulfilling prophecy, do you choose partners or friends who are emotionally unavailable? Can you give examples?

CONFRONTING PERSONAL BELIEFS

Do you have a chip on your shoulder? Are you defensive? What beliefs are holding you back, making you feel resentful? (Section IX will throw valuable light on these demons.)

_____

_____

_____

_____

Parents can't always provide all your needs – but of course, it's not possible when you are a child to understand that. Children always remember what their parents *didn't* do for them. What did your parents *not* do for you? Do you feel short-changed? Remember, this is coming from an idealistic, imaginative, literal child's point of view. My simple personal example: I had written at the top of my Christmas present list for several years that I wanted a box of 72 Derwent pencils. Every year, I received a box of 36 Derwents and one year a box of 24. It's funny what we remember, isn't it?

_____

_____

_____

_____

Now that you have exposed your belief, what can you do to support your inner child now? For example, I bought myself a box of 72 Derwent pencils and still love them! Perhaps we really are big kids at heart.

_____

_____

_____

_____

What were you told as a child to keep you in line? Are you keeping yourself in line today?

What do you believe about yourself? Is it true? Do you have any real, up-to-date proof?

What needs to be changed to get you moving forward?

Do you allow mean-spirited comments to cast a shadow over your light? Who does this to you? *Think about this.* How do they benefit by keeping you stunted and in line?

Do you believe you have choices? Some choices? No choices? Why?

_____

_____

_____

_____

Believing in yourself is the beginning of your empowered world. Is belief in yourself a difficult concept for you? Can you name your reasons? What needs to change to turn this around?

_____

_____

_____

_____

What you believe about yourself and your world runs your life. Review your responses to these questions from time to time. Remember: we always do what we believe. These are the foundations of our life and the basis of everything we are and everything we do.

Positive beliefs and thoughts give you lovely strong energy. Feed yourself strength in your thinking. Give your energy to things that are important, and don't get caught up in your monkey mind. Turn off your energy leaks with powerful thoughts.

Chapter 36

Building your powerful arsenal

Although the literal childhood model is behind you now, there will always be lingering self-doubts – and, of course, your constant companion: fear.

Your powerful arsenal is a combination of intellectual and emotional intelligence, enabling you to persist in your endeavours. It will allow you to go above and beyond anything you have ever imagined was possible for yourself, up until now.

First, find something that is close to your heart – something that is important to you; a passion. It could be a cause, a vision, or an injustice that needs to be corrected. What do you want? What do you care about so much that you are willing to risk failure, rejection and embarrassment as you push past fear, the 'order' of conformity and all the limits drummed into you when you were a child – regardless of whether you will be criticised, judged or experience any consequences coming from Centre Management?

Whatever it is, you need the full weight of your passion and iron-clad reasons to go the distance. Trust me: a burning desire to succeed will overcome the difficulties on your path. Allow me to give you a personal example.

I had written my first book, *Empowered – Secrets of Your Inner Child*. I was so enthusiastic! I couldn't wait to get out there with this life-transforming information. I had no idea there would be so many challenges. There was an ingrained culture that viewed the inner child as BS, helped along by the 'as if' response by the ego and the intellectual brain's doubtful position. All those views placed the inner child in the realm of fairy tales – therefore, the author must be a 'wanker'! ☺

It took dedication to go against the status quo and stay connected to my passion; it was my belief in my book and its powerful secrets that allowed me to go the distance. Now, of course, with *Empowered and Defiance* on the market, 'life education' concepts are being accepted more readily as they begin to make sense of and empower people's lives. Without passion, I doubt I would have persisted. Passion gives you extraordinary courage and power!

Now, let's talk about courage. What does courage mean to you? What qualities do you need to feel courageous? Highlight or circle any of the following words that bring you closer to your meaning of courage:

- resolute
- passionate
- determined
- gutsy
- enthusiastic
- patient
- persistence
- steadfastness
- brave
- heroic
- vigorous
- stamina
- tenacious
- perseverance
- willingness

Any others?

_____
_____

Passion, persistence and dedication are your new allies. What's your passion? Is there anything missing from your life that is causing you pain?

_____
_____
_____

Where or how can you make a difference? What's the gap you wish to fill?

_____
_____
_____

What beliefs do you have about success?

_____
_____
_____

What beliefs do you have about failure?

_____
_____
_____

Can you see that the risk of failing may also be a step closer to succeeding?

_____

_____

_____

It is an exciting time figuring out your life's direction and the sequential moves to get you there; a dedicated, persistent, passionate purpose gives you extraordinary courage and power!

Chapter 37
Character-building behaviours

I decide if it's important enough for me to speak up, and whether I'll regret it if I don't.

They are my decision-makers. If 'yes' to both, I formulate my plan and go quietly into action.

As I've mentioned many times, liking yourself and self-acceptance will inspire you to create a more meaningful and satisfying life. Everything you feel and believe about yourself and your life is connected to the opinion you have of yourself. Your world will change when you change. Becoming the 'mover and shaker' of your world is incredibly life-enhancing. The first inklings of your personal power produce subtle changes; your significance in your life is beginning.

Each time you take a positive step forward you will feel stronger as you sense another victory for your personal power.

Everything becomes possible and easier as you learn to lean on your inner strength for your emotional support.

There are many tiny steps you can take to begin your strengthening process. For example, you could start with something as simple as, 'No, I'm sorry. It's not possible at the moment'. That tiny sentence can do wonders for you, but you need to remain resolute. Or, you could use this one: 'I love having you in my life, and I appreciate your advice, but I need to make my own decisions. Thank you for your concern'. At the same time, a light physical touch on the arm of your adviser adds an effective emotional connection. It's a good start.

Saying what you need to say in a quiet, gentle and respectful manner — but at the same time delivering your message clearly — is character building at its best. No swearing, shouting or cursing allowed, or you lose! Each time you stand up, you will feel stronger.

Remember, saying what you need to say is not confrontation. It is your right and your choice to speak up on matters that are important to you.

You are now in touch with your new and burgeoning emotional *in*dependence, standing equal to any situation. I am not talking about *every* situation, but those that are important to you and/or your family.

Emotional *in*dependence and emotional maturity are the foundations of character building. They come from your inner knowing that you are okay; that you can rely on yourself and live by your terms. Self-protective behaviours such as avoidance sever ties with your personal power, making you feel powerless, anxious, vulnerable, ineffective and insecure.

Fear will always be your companion when you are breaking new ground; you know how to handle fear now. Remember, too, the first time is always the hardest.

Build on small achievements, but have a go! Perhaps you could write to the person rather than speaking to them. Sometimes this is a great place to start. I'm not talking about angry, vengeful writing (which you *never, ever* send), but agreeable words setting out your position, always conciliatory in its intention. Or, perhaps you could approach the person with your point of view on a one-on-one basis if a group situation is too big for you to imagine, just yet.

Even a thought of breaking away from an habitual behaviour is an achievement. That's the beginning. There's more on this subject in Section X: The prison break and its Chapter on self-talk.

When the time is right for you, go for it! Remember to remain calm and softly spoken. Breathe! Strong but gentle always wins and charm disarms. Be proud of yourself – it's another great step on your path to emotional *in*dependence.

I remember the first time I stood up and put my position forward. I felt sick with anxiety. I was hyperventilating and looking for a brown paper bag! But, afterwards, my feelings towards myself and my inner child were one of total relief and amazement! 'You really stood up and said that? Wow!' It was almost a surreal state. It was my emotional *in*dependence and personal power doing the talking. I was worth standing up for, at last! After the first time, I remembered how strong and in command I felt – but even more importantly, I was no longer afraid to speak up on 'our' behalf. I felt empowered and an amazing sense of accomplishment. There was no going back!

I had broken through three major emotional and psychological barriers with my inner child:

- My emotional *in*dependence was uncaged
- My inner child's need to belong was left in its wake
- Worrying about what anyone thought was no longer an issue.

'We' were now equal with all others. I was gaining a new sense of self-respect and dignity for 'the team'. Personal power added to the team achievement and our future together. There is no better feeling than when you are using your adult personal power to speak up on issues that are important to you. It is powerful! You are now on your side.

You are transcending your childhood model!

Personal power needs action to fulfil its promises. Taking charge of your life and no longer using self-protective behaviours is quite an achievement! Don't brush it off as something anyone can do – they don't! You are special.

The next Section will expand your horizons even further and release the balance of your relationships' emotional load, liberating your childhood patterns..

Section VIII: My challenges

Section IX

Lightening your emotional load

Overview		219
Chapter 38	Anger, resentments and regrets	223
Chapter 39	Naming the offenders	227
Chapter 40	'No rules' regulations	229
Chapter 41	Unlocking your patterns	232
Chapter 42	Exposing your regrets	238
Chapter 43	Self-forgiveness – a clean slate	242

Overview

The life-changing exercise of lightening your emotional load is recommended to all readers, whether you want to go slow or cut to the chase. Anger, resentments and regrets should be cleared *before* entering adult empowerment. This means no harbouring grudges; no shadows from the past involved in your reasons for exercising free will. No more handing your power over by going against someone or against conformity for the sake of it; but, rather, simply pleasing yourself.

Free will should come into play because you want something different to what is on offer – not because you are getting even with someone or being vengeful in any way. We are going after total freedom with no other agendas. This is about you going quietly about your business, doing what you need to do to progress your life. Okay?

To help you achieve this, I have rewritten this Section from *Empowered – Secrets of Your Inner Child*, without reference to the World Title Fight. Once your negative emotional load has been cleared, you are left with a sense of immunity (interesting word) and a wonderful sense of lightness. You will certainly feel rejuvenated after you have spent valuable time ridding yourself of old emotional weight which, no doubt, has been contributing to your sense of powerlessness, depressing your spirits and is more than likely responsible for the chip on your shoulder and any defensive behaviours you find yourself exhibiting. The resentment zone becomes part of your baggage.

If you have not powered up and become emotionally independent, your resentment zone continues to thrive – governing your attitude towards everything about yourself, others and your outlook on life.

Anger, resentments and regrets are among the biggest negative emotional blockages in your life. Like fear, they are your oppressors: depressing your spirit, affecting your energy, health and joie de vivre. Most destructive of all: you will never realise your true power and potential underneath all their weight!

So, what do you do with all those feelings and their damaging residue? How do you get back to a neutral or positive position?

I had tried several ways to detox my demons over the years, but nothing seemed to work (at least not for long). That was until, one day, I was sitting having a cuppa, thinking about the people and situations throughout my life that had contributed to my feelings of impotence and general dislike for myself; wondering how they could still be connected to me or influencing me in current time. I started to write how I felt offended, undermined, embarrassed and 'put upon' by those people or compromised positions. My feelings tumbled out quickly, one on top of the other. In fact, I could hardly keep up with their competitive spirit; they couldn't wait to be acknowledged!

They weren't stories. They were one-liners indicating only how I *felt*. *Bingo!* I knew I had stumbled upon something quite remarkable. After a week or so of spring cleaning, I *felt* totally liberated – lighter and, the most amazing feeling of all, at peace with myself and feeling one with my inner child – for the first time in my life!

Please don't allow this simple exercise to deter you. It was life-changing for me; I trust it will be for you, too. Your feelings will always be your friends, *especially* when they are acknowledged.

Being able to see the reasoning behind your childhood patterns will add serious power and weight to your intellectual arsenal. Let's find out how much your negative emotional load has been affecting your spirit.

Chapter 38

Anger, resentments and regrets

> *Left unacknowledged, anger, resentments and regrets taint your attitude and manifest the chip on your shoulder and defensive behaviours. They become squatters, chiselling away at your spirit, creating all kinds of mischief.*

Anger, resentments and regrets represent the uncomfortable side of life. Preferring not to own them or concede that you could feel such things does not make them go away. In fact, left unacknowledged, their increasing numbers negatively affect your attitude, further reducing your sense of power. Let's break down each component and take a closer look.

Anger

Even though anger is classified as a resentment, I have separated anger from resentments because it has higher levels of toxicity; is louder and more aggressive and has much greater intensity and energy, as we discovered in Chapter 19.

If you prefer not to use the word 'anger' or it does not sum up the feeling for you, highlight or circle any substitute words from the list over the page that resonate with you:

- annoyed
- hostile
- defeated
- irritated
- furious
- disturbed
- cheesed off
- anxious
- disrespected
- cross
- infuriated
- ruffled

- resentful
- upset
- indignant
- exasperated
- enraged
- uncomfortable
- stirred
- provoked
- incensed
- peeved
- irascible
- discomposed

Any others?

_____

_____

_____

Resentments

Resentments are all the feelings that niggle at you when you think about a particular person or situation. They are about how you felt offended or ill-treated, sometimes by those closest to you; where you believed they should have acted differently, with more kindness or understanding. Resentments are often linked to your inner child's tribal and security-based needs and your teen's need for acceptance and the subsequent feelings of powerlessness from both eras.

If you are harbouring just one or two resentments, you could rightly say they have no impact; but they build their strength in numbers over the years, affecting your attitude and reinforcing your defensive behaviours.

As with anger, perhaps the word 'resentments' is too general. You need to resonate with the word, knowing exactly what it means to you. Again, from the list below, please circle or highlight the words that most appeal to you when you think of resentments:

- dislike
- restless
- troubled
- irritated
- annoyed
- offended
- jealous
- injured
- acrimonious
- alienated
- rebellious
- belittled
- disquiet
- intimidated
- shafted
- upset
- discouraged
- insulted
- abandoned
- misjudged
- undermined
- uncomfortable
- rejected
- agitated
- melancholy
- dispirited
- despondent
- animosity
- tense
- uneasy
- anxious
- taken for granted
- used
- beaten
- disheartened
- envious
- defeated
- disrespected

Any others?

_____
_____
_____

Regrets

Regrets are personal and they impact you deeply. There are basically two types of regrets, which may be interpreted as:

1. a perceived or actual missed opportunity

2. thoughts of 'I wish I had' or 'I should have'.

A perceived missed opportunity could mean that you missed out on a promotion that you felt was due to you – they brought in an outsider!

An actual missed opportunity could be where you didn't step up and ask someone out on a date and a short time later you heard she had moved in with someone else.

'I wish I had' or 'I should have' are the churning over, 'if only' variety of regrets spurred on by anger at yourself: 'how could I be so stupid, so trusting, so fearful' and so on.

When you understand the reasons for your regrets – what caused them, what you did or didn't do – you will be fully aware next time, able to take charge of similar situations. It is powerful knowledge.

When you take the feeling of regret to heart, no matter which type, you may find it difficult to forgive yourself. 'If onlys' can last a long time, leaving their damaging residue and tormenting you with feelings of despondency and self-flagellation. They can reduce the trust you have with yourself and your trust in life generally. You need to learn from them so you can progress. As they say, 'There is genius in hindsight'.

If you live long enough, you will have regrets. You will soon know how many you are carrying around.

Chapter 39
Naming the offenders

*This exercise is not personal against 'them'.
It is personal for you to enable your free will
to enter your life with a clean slate.*

This cleansing exercise is different. It's about embracing all your negative feelings since you were a child through to present day. Remember: feelings have no logic; this is about how you *felt* and are still feeling without the veil of tribal needs, your child's security blanket or your teen's need for acceptance cloaking your feelings of powerlessness any longer. When you bring those feelings into the open, you won't believe the emotional 'stuff' you have been hoarding.

Acknowledging your disempowered feelings is a major key to unlocking your emotional freedom.

Please use your journal for this exercise. To get started, write a list of all the people in your life, as far back as you can remember, who have left you feeling offended, defensive, disrespected, humiliated, powerless – think of your own special words from the previous Chapter, too. You may like to begin your list with some members of your tribal family. Again, this is about your emotional cleansing. There is no shame and absolutely no guilt in this one, absolutely none. Not all of us had the advantage or good fortune of growing up with a loving, emotionally conscious family. So, go for it!

When you think of someone's name and you have a negative reaction, you are on the right track. It doesn't matter how many offenders there are on your list or who they are. A few may be closest to you, others may be from high school/secondary college, perhaps a coach, a neighbour from the past or present, maybe a former boss, a colleague or an ex-partner. Randomly list them just the same. Remember: this is your liberation. Make sure your name is somewhere on that list, too! The reason will soon become clearer. No-one is off the hook, until you say so. More power!

One more consideration: were there any issues, problems or circumstances you were born into that seem unfair to you? For example, expectations around your gender and career or education opportunities? Do you still feel angry or resentful about those contentious issues? If yes, please add them to your list. They could come under the heading 'Miscellaneous'. Getting those feelings out will be tremendously freeing and beneficial for you, too.

Now you have assembled your list, you can relax, as the next level of 'no rules' for this exercise is explained.

Chapter 40
'No rules' regulations

*I love 'no rules'. This is about you and your feelings;
not about 'them'! It is confidential between you,
your inner child and teenage self and your pen and paper.*

You are not going to war verbally with anyone or any situation or circumstance on your list. The whole idea is to privately air and acknowledge all your negative feelings and grievances, ultimately liberating your resentment zone and defensive behaviours.

Your lists of grievances are meant to be healthy fun, for your eyes only, helping to free you from the powerlessness of the past all the way through to present-day angst, and, at the same time, unlocking the reasons behind some of your childhood core behaviours and patterns too.

Your responsibility

There must be 100 per cent honesty with yourself. Every negative feeling you have ever felt when dealing with anyone or any situation/circumstance on your list is viable. Laugh at the absurdity. Laugh at how childish some of your feelings appear to be. Remember, many will be coming from your inner child's time zone and its fear-based boundaries and all those feelings of powerlessness and intimidation since then.

Allow your ego and logical brain to sneer; it's not about logic. Don't judge or justify any feelings or statements that come up. Allow your inner life jurisdiction. Be a child again – have fun for a while! There is nothing like venting to feel joyous! You won't believe how liberated you will feel, very soon.

How to 'set up' your offenders

You will be working through your list, one offender or circumstance at a time – writing your feelings down in bullet form – perhaps not the best choice of words! ☺

Before you start each session, make sure you have an oversupply of pens and plenty of blank pages available in your journal. Turn off your phone and make yourself comfortable. Ignore the doorbell. This is your time – honour yourself.

Journal exercise

Start a new page in your journal. Take one name from your list and write that name at the top of the page.

The statements you will be writing represent all the feelings you are carrying around with you that cause you emotional pain, distress and discomfort when you think of that person or situation. In a few words, reveal exactly how you felt or how you are feeling. Acknowledgement is the key to liberating all those feelings. Some examples:

- I resent being taken for granted by you.
- I regret not standing up to you.
- I hate the way I feel when you make fun of me in company.
- I am fed up with your expectations of me.
- I wish I had said 'no' to you.
- I should have listened to my intuition.

Let all that anger out! Allow all those resentments and regrets to surface and then release them with your blessings. There are no rules; there is no code of conduct. Be as hard-hitting as you like; hitting below the belt is more than acceptable! Use any number of expletives if that helps you, too! Allow your emotional body to give up all its secrets.

Write each grievance quickly until you have exhausted all your statements for that offender. You may think of a few more offences, which you can add later. Sometimes it can take a few sessions to rid yourself of all the debris from a relationship or a situation. That's okay, too.

You may find, as I did, that as you write your grievances, your mind won't distinguish anger from a resentment or a regret – simply write them down as they come through. At this stage, one list with all your grievances for each offender will suffice.

Save some offenders for tomorrow or whenever you choose. Allow plenty of time for each person on your list and make sure you are not tired when you start your list. Take all the time you need. There are no time limits. I took just under a week to list all my pain. It was nearly a full-time job!

Over to you … vent, vent, vent! Don't leave anything out – even the tiniest niggle has probably quadrupled in size by now. Continue to clean up and clear out, lifting all the pain and weight from your spirit. Have fun!

We'll catch up again later, after you have finished this cleansing, liberating exercise.

Chapter 41
Unlocking your patterns

You'll soon be liberating your childhood model's patterns and behavioural code of conduct.

All done?

- How are you feeling?
- Have all the offenders on your list been crossed off and dealt with?
- Did you have fun? Any laughter?
- Did you establish a 'miscellaneous' file?
- Did you feel a sense of your inner child's powerlessness or helplessness?
- Can you see how your 'need to belong' interferes with your feelings of personal power and free will?
- Can you believe all the stuff you have just unloaded?
- Are you feeling lighter?
- Do you feel a sense of relief and release from your past?
- Any tears?
- Can you see where some of your 'stuckness' comes from?
- Are you sensing a new alignment with your personal power?

You'll soon see how your emotional independence (personal power) gets tangled up with tribal and security needs and peer-group acceptance. Now, what do you do with all this information? You are about to meet your inner child's core behavioural patterns!

Firstly, get all your lists together. May I suggest you write a separate list for your regrets. The reason I am suggesting you write two lists is because both areas are based upon fear/security issues, but they are more than likely coming in from two different angles:

1. Anger and resentments are most likely caused by fear and your literal inner child's feelings of powerlessness with its underlying need to belong, and security and welfare issues — all sentiments contained in the childhood model.

2. Regrets, on the other hand, are more likely the result of fear and its related, negative 'what ifs' and the uncertainty involved with risk — all sentiments endorsed by the childhood model; those constrictions remaining 'live' when you are unaware of them.

Scanning your anger and resentments list, can you see any 'survival patterns'? They come under the inner child's security-based needs of 'I did it to belong' and 'I did it to be loved'. My guess is a large percentage of items on your anger and resentments list come under these two needs. Here are some of the survival patterns and security needs I uncovered for myself:

- 'I need to stay out of trouble'
- 'I need to remain passive to belong'
- 'I need to always appear fair and reasonable'
- 'I need to avoid expressing myself, so I don't upset anyone'.

Would you like to summarise your interpretations of your child's tribal-based security needs in your journal?

You are now accessing your feelings of powerlessness and seeing the ways you have 'knuckled under' in return for your survival and sense of security. This is another unconscious, reciprocal bargaining agreement. As you now know, the idea of not being cared for or being abandoned is terrifying to a child. Your inner child's motives are so pure and simple, aren't they?

The fact is: now you are an adult, you may no longer feel the need to be so obliging!

The following is a summary of my core behaviours relating to belonging and security. All were liberating but those marked *bingo!* were the ones most liberating for me. I am now willing to release:

- My need for patterns
- My need to belong – as a child
- My feelings of powerlessness – to belong
- My need to appear fair and reasonable – to be loved
- My need to feel I must be accepted – to belong *(Bingo!)*
- My need to be cared for
- My need not to question an authority figure – to belong
- My need to avoid *(Bingo!)*
- My need to be so trusting
- My painful need to appear perfect – to belong *(Bingo!)*
- The anger I have felt towards myself for never feeling I was enough *(Bingo!)*.

Would you like to create a similar summary of your belonging and security behaviours that you are now willing to release?

The following statements summarise my new conscious adult position:

- 'I no longer need anyone's approval to feel okay about myself'
- 'I have rights and I make my own choices'
- 'I am no longer controlled by my inner child's concepts and limitations'
- 'I am *not* here to live up to the expectations of others'
- 'I am an individual with my own unique style. I will be true to myself'
- 'I am here to live up to my potential'
- 'I now take full responsibility for my life'

Would you like to draw up a similar summary from your anger and resentments list, indicating where you are today and how you will live your life from now on? Did you recognise any areas you can work on that could make your life easier?

Did you establish a 'Miscellaneous' file? What did you discover? Is it the way your powerless inner child saw itself? With new intellectual insights, what is now possible? Did you identify any patterns that left you feeling powerless? Did you see any 'should' patterns you are willing to set free? Seeing the mechanics of your literal child's brain at work, trying to make sense of its tiny world, is amazing, isn't it?

Are you willing to release the need for patterns in your life?

How will your tribal and generational need to belong, now conscious, transform into your personal power? (What a fabulous question!)

Are there any resentments or anger you are not willing to release – just yet? These are your grudges. Grudges take a long time to heal. It would be a good idea if you wrote yourself a separate list of your grudges in your journal. You know those wounds won't heal without acknowledging how hurt you have been by someone's actions or ill treatment of you. Letting go of old grudges is enormously empowering – reducing their weight and lightening your attitude. Great work!

The following list summarises what I learnt about myself; once again, those marked *bingo!* were the most meaningful and liberating:

- 'I am powerful in my own right'
- 'I am beginning to feel okay about myself'
- 'I am beginning to like the new me' *(Bingo!)*
- 'I can heal now'
- 'I will speak up on matters important to me' *(Bingo!)*
- 'I will write my books. They will help lots of people and give them hope' *(Bingo!)*
- 'I have lots of choices'
- 'I am still a work in progress and will continue to be so for the rest of my life'
- 'I am feeling successful' *(Bingo!)*
- 'I can move forward with hope and inspiration'
- 'It's definitely time for change'.

What have you learnt about yourself by acknowledging your anger and resentments? Use my list above as your example, if you wish.

They say the past always catches up with us; but this time, you have turned the tables and you are catching up with your past, voluntarily!

Great work!

You may like to take some time to digest and dwell on your discoveries. Think about what you have just accomplished. What will your life look like now?

We'll catch up with your regrets when you are ready.

Chapter 42
Exposing your regrets

Unconsciously basing your decision-making on your literally perceived childhood model beliefs, places enormous constrictions upon your sense of choices and possibilities — while trying to get it right in current time. Cut yourself some slack. Considering all the handicaps, you have done very well.

Before you began this exercise, did you sometimes feel it was you against the world? I know I did sometimes. Now it's time to retrieve your list of regrets, whether separated from your anger and resentments list or not. Can you tell the difference between your perceived or actual missed opportunities and your 'I wish I had' or 'I should have', explained in Chapter 38? How many of your regrets were perceived or actual missed opportunities? Can you categorise them?

Now let's examine your 'I wish I hads' and 'I should haves'. What do you see? Did some begin their life as anger or perhaps a resentment then crossed over into a regret? Where do they fit now?

As I mentioned previously, regrets generally occur when we have felt intimidated by fear or negative 'what ifs' when the uncertainty involved in risk stopped us from taking the next step. Regrets are usually tinged with self-flagellating anger. Regrets are hard on all of us and they are difficult to accept. But their upside is that they are your lessons and you have an opportunity to use this powerful new knowledge about yourself to work *on* your life, rather like an overview, instead of from the standard perspective of working *in* your life where it's difficult to see the forest from the trees. Congratulations!

Have a think about how this information might assist in your future decision-making opportunities. For example, you might make some of the following promises to yourself:

- 'I will set boundaries for myself with others when I feel they are necessary'
- 'I will question my fear-based responses and why I am holding back'
- 'I will base my decisions on well-considered "big picture" knowledge'
- 'I will ask more questions'
- 'I won't be pushed into making major decisions within someone else's timeframe – I will take my time'
- 'I will be more discriminating with my trust'
- 'I will trust my instincts and the beliefs I have in myself'
- 'I will reconcile whether my fears are childhood perceived or actual fears'.

Keep your list of promises handy. It will put you in the right mindset when the next opportunity to practise 'putting yourself first' comes your way. No doubt you will refer to this list regularly, until it becomes a habit.

Could these lists help you in other areas of your life too? How?

_____
_____
_____
_____

How do you feel about your relationship with yourself now? What changes are possible for you? Are you willing to cut yourself some slack?

_____
_____
_____
_____

Are you beginning to feel a new sense of power over your childhood comfort zones and boundaries?

_____
_____
_____
_____

There's a lot to go up against, isn't there? When you don't understand where your pressures are coming from, or if you make a quick decision to alleviate those pressures, all your fears and old boundaries contained in your child's model rule your decision-making.

Your feelings have done their job. With this new information, how do you imagine your life will change for you?

_____

_____

_____

You are winning with your new understanding of your childhood patterns, winning with yourself and winning with your life on many levels – secretly realising you are okay. Truly believe that you have taken a giant leap towards your liberation, your new consciousness and your personal power. Your life is very much in your immensely capable hands now. You are well on your way to exquisite free will.

It should be noted that you can use this form of exercise whenever you feel your emotional life needs a spring clean. It's a great way of rejuvenating your spirit, too.

Chapter 43

Self-forgiveness – a clean slate

Forgiveness is not about allowing anyone off the hook; it's about lightening up and letting yourself off the hook.

Please write yourself a letter of forgiveness – for your eyes only. This will help you to release any old feelings of blame, shame, guilt, feeling like a victim or any other derogatory feelings you may have felt about yourself. Again, please use your journal.

This was a big one for me – letting go of all the old, disapproving feelings I had built up towards myself. Self-forgiveness adds enormously to your feelings of self-acceptance and liking who you are today, helping to heal your inner child and allowing a new sense of empowerment with your complete and evolving team effort. It is the beginning of your new future, freeing you to walk your own path.

Continue to spring clean your anger, resentments and regrets as they appear until all that is left is peace and love for your inner child and yourself.

Section IX: My challenges

Section X
The prison break

Overview		247
Chapter 44	Emotional expansion – your courage shopping List	249
Chapter 45	Self-talk	252
Chapter 46	The impostor	258
Chapter 47	Fear and conformity vs emotional independence and free will	263

Overview

We'll begin this Section with your courage shopping list. What do you want? How would you like to live? Where would you like to live? What do you want to do? What do want to have in your life more than anything else? This list should be assembled with a sense of light-heartedness and a willingness to 'think big'.

Positive self-talk is a great fear diffuser. Rather like a coach with his skilful coaxing, positive self-talk can build your confidence, allowing the more tentative part of your nature to develop strong emotional and belief muscles. As you create more mindful and intentional strength, it is possible to generate new behaviours with the support of strong, powerful self-talk energy.

Becoming an impostor is a strategy that allows you to use your adult resourcefulness and ingenuity in a light-hearted way to overcome any obstacles relating to your blossoming confidence. It is a continuation of your personal power and your right to use free will.

Chapter 44
Emotional expansion – your courage shopping list

What would you really love to do or achieve in your lifetime? Take your dreams from improbable to possible then actual.

Let's continue Marianne Williamson's beautiful quotation from her book *A Return to Love:*

> Your playing small does not serve the world. There is nothing enlightened about shrinking so that other people will not feel insecure around you. We are all meant to shine, as children do.

Forget boundaries, override all the things you were told you can't do or you can't have – or that you told *yourself* you can't do and you can't have! – and write a list of things you would like to do or have in your life. Include things you may consider imaginary or unobtainable! Really sound like and act like a *defiant* brat as you compose your list!

Perhaps you can leave this question in plain view for the next week or so and just allow your thoughts and ideas to come through freely. Nothing is out of the question, even if you secretly think it's unachievable or impracticable ... write it down. Stay light-hearted.

Project manage your life. See your life as something you are building. Concentrate on one item from your list at a time. Visualise the result first, then retrace your steps from the result to where you are now. List the steps you need to take to bring the item on your list into your life. Keep your target in focus first thing in the morning, throughout the day and just before you go to sleep.

Note: happiness is *not* future oriented. Happiness enters your life in present time when you are in the pursuit of 'something' you desire – 'something' you are working towards. This also correlates with the expression, 'It's the journey, not the destination', so really enjoy creating those steps and following them through.

Remember: your thoughts injected with passion are like magnets. Like attracts like. What you are searching for is also searching for you. Question your subconscious – get it involved. It will try its best to get you everything you want. Impress it with your passion; you are joining its frequency. Your subconscious mind wants to work for you. Give it something to do. It loves repetition. Its characteristics have been compared to a six-year-old child. Warning: be careful what you wish for – remember, your subconscious is serious and literal.

Be open to receiving anything and everything you are asking for – it may manifest in a different way to your imagination, so stay alert. If you wish to investigate the art of manifesting or invocation further, there are some really interesting books that can help you.

I shall share one of my courage shopping list success stories in the last Chapter of this Section so you will know how victorious it feels when you conquer your fears and win your inner battle.

Chapter 45

Self-talk

Motivating, inspiring and coaching yourself to success is the voice of personal power! Affirming self-talk is an exercise with enormous power and potential. It is portable, available 24/7 – whenever you need some reassuring encouragement.

Slowly, as I became conscious, I began to accept that my adult self was more than capable of providing my own security without the burden of certainty; and that my capabilities far outweighed anything my inner child could have imagined for itself, or me!

However, I needed a way of bridging the gap between where I was and where I wanted to be. I needed to feel uplifting support that would enable me to live up to my potential and reach the next rung in my development.

Positive self-talk filled the gap! I had found my reassuring push to give me the encouragement to try. Self-talk is a powerful ally; it really works and it can be very inspiring. It is a great and easy form of confidence-building, helping to overcome emotional hurdles and obstacles on your path relating to security issues and challenges generally.

You are on the brink of a life-changing approach to the way you handle your personal affairs, especially fear and self-doubt. Positive self-talk will bring out the best in you. It will:

- give you the encouragement to try
- motivate and inspire you
- coach and coax you
- praise your efforts
- acknowledge your achievements
- help you work with and on your fears from childhood and beyond
- help you to open yourself and your inner child to a new world of possibilities.

Positive self-talk can be likened to the way a paramedic speaks softly and gently to someone needing their support. It is a delightful, reassuring technique that can be applied to all kinds of situations in your life, including encouraging your children and others. Self-talk will help to ensure your continuing progress.

Trying is your new success – regardless of the outcome.

The concept of failure is a unique human concept. Animals don't understand the word 'failure'. They have never been shown nor have they felt failure. They don't know the feeling of embarrassment or intimidation. They just keep trying until they get what they want, by staying focused.

Mastering the art of affirming self-talk

To use self-talk successfully, you need to become aware of your internal dialogue, i.e. the words and phrases you use every day when speaking to yourself. Examine them. Write them down in your journal if you like. Are they powerful, positive, affirming words and phrases or do they leave you feeling despondent, powerless and negative? Your choice of words and phrases can help boost your beliefs in yourself, impacting on the type of future you are making for yourself now, taking your image to the next level, too.

You may also like to go back and check the words you chose in Chapter 4: Building a courageous self-image. Are these words big enough now? We'll review them again in Chapter 48.

Now let's add a few positive, self-affirming phrases to your chosen powerful words. You know what works for you! You know what you need to hear to empower yourself! Highlight your chosen lines from any of the following to get you started and in the mood:

- 'I love taking charge of my life.'
- 'I know where I'm heading, and I can't wait to take the next step.'
- 'My fears are perceived fears. They can't hurt me.'
- 'I'm planning my future now.'
- 'Old beliefs tremble when they see me coming!'
- 'I love conquering my fears.'
- 'I am building big reserves of … for my future.'
- 'I am emotionally strong and getting stronger.'
- 'I love directing my life.'
- 'My fears and self-doubts are mostly a delusion from my childhood.'
- 'I feel comfortable with my new image.'
- 'I am working towards my emotional independence.'
- 'I love feeling fit in all different ways.'

- 'I feel my life turning around in my favour.'
- 'I have never felt so alive and in control.'
- 'I feel ready to take on more responsibility for my future.'
- 'I am okay with the concept of impermanence.'
- 'I am working towards my financial independence.'
- 'I accept that I hold the keys to my future.'
- 'I love using my ingenuity to overcome challenges in my life.'
- 'I am overriding my childhood self-doubts.'
- 'Security is no longer a necessity or an issue for me.'
- 'I am becoming used to the idea of uncertainty.'
- 'I love the idea of challenging my ingenuity.'
- 'My intentions are my word.'
- 'I adapt to change easily.'
- 'I love that my life is in my very capable hands.'
- 'I am ready and willing to go beyond my childhood limits.'
- 'I am bigger than this situation. We can do this!'
- 'I am capable of achieving anything I want in my life.'
- 'There is nothing hard about this. Let's make it happen!'
- 'I am motivated and inspired.'
- 'I am totally responsible for my life and loving it.'
- 'I have never felt so free.'
- 'Passion, persistence and dedication win!'
- 'I am a winner!'
- 'I am so much more than I ever thought possible.'
- 'I am much stronger emotionally than I ever thought I could be.'

- 'My attitude has never been better.'
- 'I am emotionally equipped to handle anything that comes my way.'
- I am now ready, willing and able to face my future with new confidence.'

Would you like to add your own motivational phrases?

_____

_____

_____

_____

I have used this method frequently. Self-talk builds rapport between you, your inner child and wherever you are heading. It takes you to the next level with inspiration, encouragement and stronger feelings of 'Yes, I can do this!' It is an attitude changer. You are becoming your own life coach!

Regular use of positive self-talk will help you to overcome fear, self-doubt and your inner child's insecurities and need for certainty. Continue to encourage yourself; talk gently, softly and lovingly to your inner child: 'Come on kiddo, I know we can do this! We are a great team'.

Remember: this is simply about you using your personal power and becoming conscious and responsible for everything that is happening in your life today. You are deciding what is right for you, and where and how you fit into this world. Creative self-talk is your self-help strategy.

Newness keeps you alive and thriving. Encourage yourself through positive self-talk to try new things and develop new ideas. You stand equal to everything that comes your way. You are one step closer to whatever it is you want. And, know this: with some encouraging self-talk, there is nothing that you are not capable of figuring out and going after.

You are becoming one with your new confidence level, aligned and ready to meet your future. There is nothing you can't do when you put your heart and your mind into it and support yourself with positive self-talk. Working with your emotional nature, your talents will rise to the top like cream. As you take ownership of your life and move forward at your own pace with passion, determination, courage and persistence – there will be no stopping you.

Congratulate yourself regularly on your continuing progress. It's amazing – *you're amazing*! Look how far you have travelled since you began your journey ... and there's more!

Chapter 46
The impostor

Trying out new roles can be scary. Venturing into the unknown can bring up old stories and fear from your childhood model subconscious responses.

Sometimes the thought of standing on your own – for example, saying something like, 'X is not acceptable to me' and defying your old feelings of powerlessness – can be extremely stressful. I remember my first experiences; I was hyperventilating at the thought!

When you haven't incorporated 'the who' you feel on the inside with 'the who' you appear to be on the outside, you need a way to connect those two worlds. When you are somewhere between those two identities, you can impose yourself on your behaviour and act 'as if' or 'fake it till you make it' (as they say) during this transition. I have chosen to use 'the impostor' as the stage caricature. Again, light-heartedness is the key.

What is an impostor? To set the scene, let's look at a few words, as we usually do, that could be substituted for the word 'impostor':

- actor
- imitator
- fraudster
- poser
- mimic
- pretender
- masquerader
- illusionist
- disguiser

It has been established that an impostor is someone who pretends to be someone or something else. In this scenario, it is about you allowing your 'impostor' image to take centre stage and bring the seemingly disparate positions of how you feel versus who you appear to be together, harmoniously – through the use of the impostor. The impostor knows no boundaries. It is available for use in *all* situations.

You will soon see how small and frightened your inner child's world really is. Your inner child's primal need is to survive, so he will do whatever it takes to give himself that sense of safety and security. Your inner child manufactured, by instincts and feelings, a safe haven. If he leaves his comfort zones, how will he survive? Fear creates the boundaries around this concept by reminding you every time you step away from its safety net, that you are breaking its boundaries. In other words, you have two fearful reminders trying to stop you from advancing!

Here are some examples of the possible dialogue between your inner child and fear both trying to stop you, and the impostor – you – as you override their warnings and advance your position:

Child: 'I don't need success. I want to stay here. I want to feel okay!'

Fear: 'You know you'll be found out, don't you? Don't you feel apprehensive? Uneasy?'

You: 'Thank you for your warnings but I have worked diligently; I am worthy of success and I'm accepting this promotion on our behalf.'

Child: 'I don't want recognition. It scares me!'

Fear: 'What a fraud you are! Can't you feel your anxiety?'

You:	'I do feel anxious, but I deserve recognition and appreciation for all my efforts. I'm accepting the recognition on our behalf.'
Child:	'I don't deserve such high praise.'
Fear:	'I'm here to warn you! Feel my warnings! You will be found out!'
You:	'Trust me, I am fearful. I'm learning on the job and I accept the praise for my work. It's good to advance our position.'
Child:	'Why can't we just stay here? Everything is okay here.'
Fear:	'You need to stay in line! Don't extend your boundaries! I'm keeping you safe.'
You:	'I know you are trying to keep me safe, but I need to try. Trying means we are moving forward and closer to success.'
Child:	'I'm okay the way I am. Who'll look after me if you give your heart to someone else?'
Fear:	'I'm trying to keep you out of harm's way! I'm in your DNA. Can't you feel the fear?'
You:	'I know you are trying to protect us, but this new relationship is special. I intend to take care of all of us.'
Child:	'What about me? Why can't it just stay the same? I'm frightened!'
Fear:	'What happens when you cross the line? I won't be able to protect you there.'
You:	'I know I'm taking a chance, but I need to expand my boundaries. I trust and believe I can handle it. It's for our future.'

Child:	'I don't need all this attention. I want to stay out of the spotlight.'
Fear:	'You need to obey me! I'm here to keep you safe. Can't you feel how anxious you are?'
You:	'Yes, I do feel stressed and anxious, but I work smart and diligently. We deserve our success.'
Child:	'I don't need success. I'm okay the way I am.'
Fear:	'You must be on something if you think you can pull this off! Stop before you make a fool of yourself.'
You:	'I know I'm going against all your warnings, but success is trying – no matter the outcome. If I don't try, how will we know?'
Child:	'I'm going to get into a lot of trouble over this. It really scares me!'
Fear:	'You will look like an idiot. You will crash and burn. Butterflies are warning you!'
You:	'I do feel uneasy but it's worth a try. I'll ask for assistance if I get stuck; they won't mind. This is for us.'
Child:	'I don't want to be forgotten. I want to stay here with you.'
Fear:	'They'll reject you! Can't you see how embarrassed you will feel? I'm saving you.'
You:	'Thank you for your concern. I went for the interview. They shortlisted me. I got the job! Yes, I am getting away with it, and no I'll always look after you.'

Can you see how the impostor is allowing you to expand your life, accepting much bigger roles and more responsibility, stepping confidently into your well-deserved new image?

So, really there is nothing to stop you from breaking free of the childhood model's imagined encumbrances. You control fear with your new adult intellectual conscious responses. You are so much more than you have ever dared to believe.

Wow ... and yes, you are getting away with it! No-one has found out yet! No-one even suspects you – because there is nothing to find out! You are now a fully fledged adult with all types of qualifications, wisdom and life education. You are above suspicion.

Chapter 47

Fear and conformity vs emotional independence and free will

Hello courage shopping list! ☺

What you are about to challenge are the beliefs contained in your childhood model's automatic subconscious responses and your teenager's generational need for conformity. You are now on a journey to breach all the rules that have been keeping you disciplined, obedient and passive – like a child.

It is your emotional life that determines the size of your life, not your IQ alone! It is a collaborative effort – yin/yang – the Chinese complete.

Your emotional life is personal. No-one else's emotional life is holding you back. No-one else feels the way you do, has your background, or understands your motives, motivation or passion. You are unique and you are emotionally unique.

> **Understand that fear and your 'need to belong' are the culprits that continue to lock you into emotional conformity issues. You are now searching for a 'break-out-of-jail' card.**

The following example is taken directly from an item on my courage shopping list to give you an indication of exactly what I am referring to when I mention courage shopping. I invite you to join me on my journey into *adult defiance*, pushing fear-based emotional boundaries and choosing quiet, exquisite free will to victory. ☺

In June 2017 as I was driving down the highway, I watched as the sexiest, most stunning black car drove past me. 'OMG – what was that?!' I exclaimed out loud. I followed that car! The model, which turned out to be the latest, did not name the car. All I could see was 'GT' on its boot. I followed it along the busy highway, quickly drove in front of it to get a good look at the front view, where I caught sight of the 'Mustang' badge on the grill. Ah-ha! Then I drew alongside to get a close-up of its side view. By then, the driver knew exactly what I was doing and smiled at my enthusiasm – probably reminding him of his 'love at first sight' attraction to the car, too.

A few days later, I noticed a red Mustang driving towards me. When I got home, champing at the bit by then, I checked Google to discover that Ford had released Mustangs onto the Australian market a year or so earlier, but there had been quite a wait between order date and delivery. The first Mustang I saw was more than likely one of the first of those imports.

I couldn't believe how much I wanted one of those cars, especially as I had never really been a car enthusiast, let alone a petrol head! Nevertheless, I read lots of reviews and no matter the comments, my heart knew I had to have one. All my senses were under its spell. I was in love!

Fear, of course, was in the midst of all this passion putting up all kinds of anxious barriers and emotional obstacles as to why I shouldn't go ahead with the purchase, as it tried, in vain, to change my heart's desire.

I had to get some work done on my garage before I allowed myself to seriously re-consider overriding my fear of ridicule, embarrassment and rejection, such as:

- 'Why would a woman of your age, and a grandmother of six, buy a Mustang? You will look ridiculous! Grow up, Louise!'
- 'What will your neighbours, family, friends and daughters think or say?'

The most embarrassing thought of all – the one that almost stopped me from going ahead – was 'Mustang Sally'. My fears again came in quickly with the thought, 'What's the world coming to? Don't you have any dignity?' (Apparently not!)

I ordered a set of personalised Mustang plates that sat in all their glory on my desk, acting as my co-conspirator spurring me on.

Remember, it is your subconscious responses and fear that are putting forward all the reasons why you shouldn't break old boundaries. And remember, too, that fear is meant to control you, keeping you small, in line and emotionally contracted. Of course, fear has its uses and its place, but not when you want a Mustang!

Regardless of all those fearful reminders and intimidation, my heart and my right to make my own choices eventually won and I made the gargantuan decision to go ahead and order my Mustang, with precisely the colour and features I wanted. Exactly one month later, there I was sitting in the driver's seat of a sparkling, brand-new oxford white 5.0 litre V8 fastback coupe, complete with specially ordered nickel-plated wheels and my set of personalised Mustang plates. I took the keys to my triumphant emotional expansion, not worrying about or concerning myself (*too* much) with whether I belonged or not! More obstacles overcome on my path to heroism – in my eyes. I named my car 'The Legend', reinforcing its reputation and secretly thinking I was a kind of a Legend, too!

My unbridled joy in this moment was not about buying the car as much as it was about my emotional freedom to choose whatever I wanted, no longer contained in the beliefs of my subconscious mind about what a woman of 'my age' should or shouldn't be doing. It was huge for me! At last, Louise was growing up! I was breaking through fear and the huge emotional barriers introduced into my subconscious mind long ago. I was no longer held back by the dictates of old beliefs or the views of my tribe or generation. And I had overcome another major hurdle by going outside my need to remain small to belong. I suddenly felt heroic!

Although I admit to initially feeling intimidated by the power and look of 'The Legend', my self-image was now liberated to the point where I felt I was at the beginning of 'all things possible' for me – bold, at last. Now, every time I sit in my car and touch the ignition button, my senses light up, producing an automatic smile. I love the sound of the big powerful engine, the look of its long, sexy, sculptured bonnet and the pride I have in myself for winning against fear and old beliefs, enabling me to live a more passionate, personalised and fulfilled life!

I am no longer a carbon copy of my childhood model, its fear and beliefs. The act of buying my Mustang has certainly rejuvenated my spirit. I can now use that example for my next emotional expansion episode and the next, ad infinitum. Is there something on your mind? Is it on your courage shopping list? I'll give you a minute to write it down.

For the record, I did receive a few disparaging remarks – in among the 'wow, good on you' variety – some from older men and men from my generation and, surprisingly, even some younger men. My daughters were evenly divided in their opinion, too: one thought it ridiculous and embarrassing, while the other was out there bragging to her friends that her mum drives a Mustang. The moral of the story:

It is not possible to please everyone, so pleasing yourself is the best and only answer.

People who object to anyone displaying the freedom of emotional expression and independence from 'the group' and its psychology, generally have not reached a stage in *their* development where they have liberated themselves from the beliefs contained in their childhood model. No doubt fear and its many affiliates are still running their lives and that powerful need to belong to their generation's conformity issues must be all-pervasive, too. Remember this: it is *their* attitude to your independence and emotional freedom that is creating the problems for them. If they say, 'Good on her', you'll know they are accepting of their adult rite of passage, too.

Positive, gentle independence has an air of dignity and elegance. You are winning on all levels with yourself and your life, overcoming old emotional barriers and that powerful, menacing need to belong. You are employing skills from your adult repertoire of behaviours to remove the obstacles on your path to freedom. Quiet, determined free will is seductive. The more you rejuvenate your spirit, the more likely you are to employ and enjoy the process as life becomes easier for you. You are living your life your way. This is where *you* are heading!

You are not fuelling the fire within, creating more drama in your life; you are allowing its simmering heat to melt old barriers. Well done! That is how I would love you to *feel* about yourself at the end of this book.

Note: logic did not come into my reasons to buy a Mustang – not even once! It was a 100 per cent emotional purchase. Emotional expansion, emotional expression and emotional independence felt great and it still feels great! I take the car out for a run frequently and enjoy every moment.

One more thing: you are not responsible for what 'others' may think of you or about you, or their attitude towards you. Opinions are mercurial: they come and go like the fads of fashion. There's lots of jealousy out there, too.

Please do not allow anything that is out of your control to control you.

Be mindful of your spirit and how it is feeling. Is your spirit nice and high?

Section X: My challenges

Section XI

Flourishing away from 'centre'

Overview		273
Chapter 48	Reviewing your powerful new ID	275
Chapter 49	Emotional maturity	278
Chapter 50	The right to be yourself	283
Chapter 51	An independent mindset	285
Chapter 52	A tribute to the adult spirit	287
Coda		289

Overview

We begin this Section with a review of Chapter 2 (your meaning of security) and Chapter 4 (the words you chose to sum up your courageous self-image). Let's find out if your chosen meanings at the beginning of this book are still the right fit for you, or whether they require adjustments in line with your evolving version of personal power and free will.

In this Section we'll also touch on emotional maturity and what that means to your expanding potential, acknowledging that the emotionally mature person rationalises and accepts the burden of responsibility towards himself, the right to be himself and to make decisions in favour of his emotional freedom – above the need to belong.

Emotional maturity is the last to acquiesce, yielding with good grace only after you have shown a willingness to allow your heart and mind to experience a world of collaboration: negotiating our considerable differences, while moving forward independently. It is your personal power in action – a celebration of emotional expression and emotional expansion – the adult affirming the right to be himself.

From this elevated position, you gain a profound understanding of the monumental progress you have made on your journey into yourself.

Chapter 48

Reviewing your powerful new ID

How big is your world today?

Let's begin by checking the answers you wrote in Chapter 2: Identifying with your sense of security. In that Chapter, I asked the following questions: '*How* do you need to feel secure?' and '*What* do you need in your life to feel secure?'

Are there any areas in your answers you now wish to change or delete?

_____

_____

_____

Can you identify any key areas that were blocking you from moving forward?

_____

_____

_____

What is your position today on your 'need to belong'?

_____
_____
_____
_____

Now, let's review your answers to the questions in Chapter 4: Building a courageous self-image. This will be the most telling of all. Have a look at the key words you used to describe yourself: do you want to delete or replace any of the words you chose? Why/why not?

_____
_____
_____
_____

Who are you aspiring to be? Are there any changes you would like to make to the words you chose? Why/why not?

_____
_____
_____
_____

Have you adjusted any of your 'image builders'? How and why?

_____
_____
_____
_____

Any other changes?

How do you see yourself and your possibilities now?

Chapter 49
Emotional maturity

The difference between an adult who is aligned with his consciousness and in touch with his independence and free will, and the adult who is not, is emotional maturity. You can sense his dignity and commanding presence.

Emotionally mature people have reached a state of self-acceptance and self-respect. There is a deep knowing and a belief that they are okay; they are self-assured. You can *feel* their power and their presence. It is awesome. Great credits on their life's CV!

There will always be problems in relationships and all situations where one or more parties remain in childhood mode. When you are trying to deal with people who are defensive, taking life personally and seriously and wanting everything to be their way, who live by the rules and refuse to negotiate outcomes or see others' points of view, you now know where they are in their development. This proposition makes it easier to understand why you can have such a battle with some people, doesn't it? Trying to deal with, say, a 50-year-old who remains in the 'personal' world of his childhood and whose emotional development has not progressed, can be very frustrating and challenging, making everyone's life – including the 50-year-old's – so much more difficult.

In *Empowered – Secrets of Your Inner Child* Section 2: The childhood maze and Section 6: Your belief system, powerful light was beamed on our amazing differences and why it's so difficult (or even impossible) to agree and progress without conciliatory responses.

Entry into adulthood has always been defined by age – that's the easy part. What about emotional maturity? How and where does that fit in?

What is emotional maturity?

The spirit of emotional maturity is centred around a willingness to let go of your child's need to feel secure and anchored to its fear-based, inflexible positions and behaviours. It is the adult rising above the ego and fear, progressing from the personal world of a child into a new, malleable emotional expression and expansion. It is about possibilities based upon choices – *your* choices. It is your personal power at work.

Your emotional life is the backbone of your life.

Emotional maturity is a new formula. It is your reward for years of living vicariously under your inner child's jurisdiction, in subservient and fixed positions. It represents a positive change in your attitude and maturing flexibility.

Embracing conciliatory responses

Before proceeding further, let's align with a few words that sum up where you are heading. Basically, it is a feeling of being comfortable and secure within yourself, relaxed in your personal power, enticing you into the possibilities of grey or conciliatory positions.

Which of the following words appeal to you?

- negotiating
- cooperating
- bargaining
- dealing
- consulting
- liaising
- agreeing
- conciliating
- harmonising
- collaborating
- compromising
- unifying

Negotiation and conciliation embrace a truly mature and evolved world where you allow your differences to become transparent, considered and negotiated. It is a win-win proposition.

Emotional maturity is where you, the adult, will be learning that your child's black-or-white, yes-or-no, can-or-can't type of childhood conditioning no longer suits your maturing, sophisticated adult world. You need more of the 'maybe', more conciliatory responses rather than the limiting one-dimensional world you may have seen, heard and imitated as a child. Emotional maturity is your willingness to work with grey options or grey areas in your life. Once again, it's about a softer edge, embracing the concept of negotiation and compromise – without *feeling* compromised. You are acknowledging there is more than one way – more than a child's safe and secure way.

When you see how much more agreeable grey positions can be, and how much more relaxed and peaceful you can feel, it is to your advantage to try to find some middle ground in your relationships – and in fact, all areas of your life – the beginning of a softer philosophy. Give and take is now a viable option.

It's exciting *not* to know outcomes before they manifest. You know you can handle uncertainty now! You have earned your guernsey.

What does emotional maturity *look* like?

Sometimes it's not until we are going grey ourselves that we become willing to acknowledge and work with grey areas. Coincidence? Here are some other ways to describe what emotional maturity can look like:

- allowing your ego and fear to have a say, but not make the ultimate decision (that's your job)
- a willingness to negotiate win–win outcomes
- being accountable for everything that is happening in your life; no blaming or avoiding
- feeling emotionally secure in your personal power
- not needing to control, own or possess anyone
- fitting in, when necessary, without holding a grudge
- feeling part of something greater than yourself
- putting forward a view, without taking it personally if it's not accepted
- allowing the other person to take the kudos if or when it's due
- conducting your life away from the resentment zone.

Any others?

_____

_____

_____

_____

_____

The emotionally mature adult sounds like a team player, doesn't it? Yes, it does – and yes, it is – the exact opposite of the ego's need to make itself feel important, superior and separate from others. You win every time you are not willing to play its head games, living by its rules.

What does emotional maturity *feel* like?

Emotional maturity brings with it a deep sense of inner security. You are an individual, separate, but united in the way you conduct your life. At peace – one with the Universe and one with your power. You can stand on the sidelines observing, free to live your life without the drama, while directing your energy into more worthwhile pursuits. From this higher position, you can confidently move forward, sensing that your spirit and soul are fully integrated and alive and that you can indeed trust yourself.

Emotional maturity is the key to living up to your highest self, setting new standards for your emotional wellbeing. You are deciding what you are willing to do for others, with no strings; whether they acknowledge you is neither here nor there, because you are acknowledging yourself.

Have no doubt, you will be given the opportunity to test your new courage, but nothing will faze you when you embrace your new inner strength. You are now on a higher frequency. The enrichment of emotional maturity is an achievement. The benefits are life-changing. You have entered the zone of a privileged few. It is a powerful place to be, and you have earned it! There is no going back. You are now in the arena of possibilities – *big* possibilities. What an incredible place to call home, and you are now 'at home' with yourself!

Chapter 50
The right to be yourself

Breathe fresh air into your life. Do whatever you need to do in this lifetime to make yourself happy. We don't have enough time to be worrying about what people may think or say about us. It's your time now.

You know you will always be judged, so why not give them something worthwhile to talk about? Please don't waste your talents. We all have talents – we were all born with something special. Perhaps you have always known deep down what it is; perhaps you felt it as a child or a teen. Do you remember having an easy talent in your childhood or teenage years? Or was there something in your younger life that you were particularly good at or loved to do; maybe there was something you secretly loved to do? It's your job to find your skill or speciality and live the dream that keeps you high on life, adding longevity as it continues to rejuvenate your spirit.

Your talent is your power base. It is usually some kind of service you render to others, giving you pleasure as you provide that service. This is called a blessing in Greek mythology. Your blessing is meant to be your life's purpose or your life's work – the source of great happiness. There may be *no* need for a tertiary qualification for this type of talent, as you gain your constantly evolving qualification via life experiences and life education. This gives the owner of this blessing humility. *Take your time and think about this.*

Perhaps you can encourage a young person in your life if you detect a natural skill. Support him and nurture his talent.

If you choose to walk your own path, remember: the greats in the history of the world – great painters, writers, architects and present-day icons – always stepped away from 'centre'. They needed to experiment, push boundaries and risk rejection for their passion. You must do the same if you wish to live independently and excel.

Today, the status quo has accepted and admires the legacy of those non-conformists who went against the 'need to conform' for a much bigger cause – the need to be themselves. Their freedom was painful, as they were ostracised or chose their own path; to remain in the fold would have been even more painful. We, the world, would never have known and added such greatness to the repertoire of human amazingness.

Chapter 51
An independent mindset

*Trust yourself, believe in yourself and be all you can be.
You deserve it all!*

You've come a long way on your journey into self-acceptance and self-reliance. You are here to honour yourself and to make the most of your gifts as you progress your life. It's time to:

- be proud of who you are today
- forget about outside acceptance
- think high thoughts about yourself
- never compare yourself to anyone
- walk your own path, moving in the direction that is right for you
- make the most of your talents, your blessings
- stay well groomed
- know you are the only one who can give you emotional nourishment
- be open and honest with yourself and others

- rely on yourself
- learn to be on your own
- be your own best friend
- never put others' importance ahead of your own
- care for yourself and make time for yourself every day
- be soft and gentle with yourself
- make things happen for you
- stay flexible in mind, body and spirit
- use your intuition, often
- realise your enormous progress
- adapt, adapt, adapt
- never say 'I can't'; say 'I'll try'
- live with a conciliatory outlook, but don't compromise yourself
- be true to yourself
- live 'I am' in your inner and outer life.

Chapter 52
A tribute to the adult spirit

No longer the adult stuck in its childhood model forever, but rather the metamorphosis into the maturing adult.

It's time to lift the sneer and scorn from philosophical notions about the midlife crisis and to elevate the position to one of admiration. In my opinion, it is the courageous adult choosing to live by his own code of behaviour, making his own emotionally independent decisions – an empowered adult who is truly congruent with his maturing existence.

Wondering what next? Why not? Some people will always be happy and want to live within their childhood model boundaries, and that is perfectly okay, too. However, I am suspecting that, having bought a book entitled Defiance, you are wanting more: wanting to find out what it feels like to live on the other side of fear and obedience! ☺

Your only limits are those beliefs formulated by you when you were under seven-years-old, and your teen's need for acceptance. Seventy-year-olds today are proving there are no limits. Mick, Keith, Charlie and Ron will never stop what they do!

They love the life they have created and it no doubt keeps them young and thriving.

Defiance – quietly detaching from conformity expectations – is reasonable and totally acceptable for the maturing adult. Carpe diem!

May I give you one more tip, from my heart to yours? Now that you understand how it all works and your part in it, please be aware that it may take several years to step into your adult power and take command of your life. It is a HUGE transition; everything takes time. Don't be hard on yourself. Cruise into your power and delight in all your experiences as you take each progressive step towards the rightful ownership of your life. Keep working on your power base every day.

Remember, happiness enters your life in present time when you are in the pursuit of 'something' you desire … 'something' you are working towards. It's the journey, not the destination.

I would like to finish this Chapter with the beautiful closing lines from Marianne Williamson's quotation:

> *As we let our own light shine, we unconsciously give other people permission to do the same.*
>
> *As we are liberated from our own fear, our presence automatically liberates others.*

Coda

No-one can *feel* exactly the way you do.

You are independent, powerful and free to make your own choices.

You are no longer a child needing permission to evolve; nor a teenager needing acceptance by its generation.

Follow your heart. Remain true to yourself.

Find your fascination; your intrigue.

Create a more 'lived-in' life.

Honour yourself.

Section XI: My challenges

Epilogue

I would like to conclude this book by taking a moment to review our relationships – particularly family relationships, as they relate so closely to the concepts explored in this book. It all begins with family.

Family respect

There seems to be a reluctance for some family units – whether they be tribal or immediate – to change with the times. This creates a widening and deepening chasm between the progress being made in the outside world and the lack of change happening within 'old' family structures.

Respect and dignity are the two prerequisites to building a healthy relationship – no matter how, when, where or why that relationship began. Without respect, what do we base our relationships upon?

★★★

I would like to touch on the large and important role families play in the context of each child's inner child and its childhood model. As you know, every child's inner child is establishing its own unique model of life. It is an unconscious, trusting, literal acceptance that whatever it is learning and observing in the first seven years of its life is real, true and correct, the way it is and the way it will always be according to the literal inner child.

Children are being shown how their new world works, especially inside the family unit. What are they learning?

- Think about the words and expressions you use when talking to or disciplining a child, or in the earshot of a child. What are they *hearing*?

- Think about the behavioural images you are displaying. What are the children learning and observing from you? What are they *seeing*?

- Think about how children feel about themselves and their capabilities in your presence. What are they *feeling*?

Children are literal. They believe and accept everything they hear, see and feel at face value. This information is being stored in their childhood model, resulting in enduring, future automatic subconscious responses.

I would also like to include teenagers. You now know they are not rebelling – they are naturally separating from you as the next stage in their development continues. In this confusing time, they need your support and understanding more than ever. Be mindful of your comments.

★★★

Open the conversation around the dinner table when most, if not all, the family members are present. Bring the above information into the dinner table conversation. Say what needs to said. Communication is the hallmark of healthy relationships. Clear the air. Speak up on matters within your family that are creating the dramas. Reduce their power. There are even advertisements with children asking their parents to stop fighting.

Are the adults setting a great example for your children, showing how people in families negotiate and conciliate their differences and end the day in harmony? Would you like your children to duplicate any of the behaviours they are seeing in your family? These are fair questions, especially when you consider the amount of feral behaviour, fear and violence being reported in some family units.

We know that the phrase 'Do as I say, not as I do!' falls on deaf ears. Children copy behaviours. The behaviours children are seeing as 'normal' will be repeated in future generations. Are there any behaviours in your family unit that are potentially damaging, creating the relationship problems of tomorrow and the next generation? We are more enlightened now. We can do better for the generations who follow us.

It is expected, at our maturing age, that we can approach this extremely important part of our lives with emotional maturity; that is, that each member of a family acknowledges the uniqueness of the other – no matter their gender, age or position. Each member should feel a sense of importance and dignity within that family group, and feel that the family is a place of safety, respect and love. *Time to break another cycle.*

★★★

Domestic violence is usually considered to be physical violence, but abuse has many tentacles. An equally powerful one, in my view, is emotional abuse – controlling, sniggering, sniping and ridiculing an individual. This type of abuse is felt on a deep emotional level; the untold damage to the psyche, self-esteem and self-worth coming through emotionally painful counselling sessions years later and perpetuating similar behaviours in the next generations before the cycle is broken.

★★★

The women's movement cannot go backwards; we cannot be expected to live the tiny lives of previous generations of women. Since World War II we have been out there, proving ourselves, slowly striving, taking ownership of our lives, expecting more of ourselves and more of our relationships, including family relationships. This expectation continues to grow and refuses to be ignored. We are acknowledging our need for respect and self-respect.

It's time to challenge old rules and conditioned behaviours. When we look at all the areas women are involved in, consummate in, all the multitasking that goes on to run a family and even more so when we are going to work every day, we cannot think of ourselves as diminutive and unimportant.

Having a family unit that does not observe and embrace this changing face of society makes it difficult to fit in within the framework of family structures that passed their 'use by' several generations ago.

We need to challenge family model basics and work with changing values, and, at the same time, review and liberate old generational issues. No-one will think less of the hierarchy taking a democratic rather than a dictatorial leadership role. In fact, that move will no doubt bolster their position, demonstrating a bold new attitude and a progressive vision for the future of families. ☺

Respectful relationships

When you decide what someone wants or needs, over and above what they have specifically decided for themselves, you are creating problems for them!

Conversely, when others decide what you want when you have already stated what is right for you, *they* are creating the problem making your life more difficult.

To compound the problem further, the situation is usually taken personally by the challenger, blaming the other – who is making his own choices – as the bad guy!

We need to step back and allow 'the other' to make their own choices, above what we believe is the right choice for them. This also applies to the parents of adult children.

Is peace on earth getting closer?

Thank you

I love being 'a slave to the quill' and I thank you for your time and commitment! You have been an inspiration to me. I hope you follow through on some of the items on your courage shopping list and *feel* your exquisite 'Mustang' freedom too. I sip to your ongoing successes and your continuing life adventure. Thank you for your trust and support; they are both very much appreciated.

Your Story

If you have a life-transforming story or one that you would like to share, perhaps including how this book changed your life, I would love to hear from you. Imagine what an inspirational book that could be for people who have all but given up or settled! Would you like to contribute? Please contact me via my website: louiselkallaway.com

Thank you.

About the author

Louise Kallaway was born in Melbourne, Australia. She has two daughters, six grandchildren and her cat, Madelyn.

Louise has been fascinated by life processes since her difficult teenage years. Her quest to unravel the mystery of life processes, particularly childhood processes and 'the system', has led her convolutedly and inadvertently to the childhood model. Her enquiring, analytical mind takes the guesswork out of the different stages of our lives, helping us to break the cycle with powerful new insights and understanding of how and why our lives don't always measure up to youthful expectations. This is the second book in her 'Life Education' series.

Louise passionately believes – as did her grandfather – that life offers its own education.

To find out more about Louise and future publications, please go to: louiselkallaway.com or www.linkedin.com/in/louise-l-kallaway - 57b667198/ or www.facebook.com/louise.kennett.58

Other books in the 'Life Education' series

Empowered – Secrets of Your Inner Child
Evolving – Secrets of a Child and Life Processes

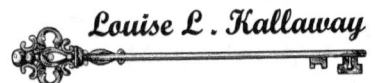

References

Chapter 3
Richard Bach, *Jonathan Livingston Seagull*, Pan Books, 1973.

Chapter 9
'The Dunedin Study', Dunedin Multidisciplinary Health and Development Research Unit, https://dunedinstudy.otago.ac.nz/studies.

The Dunedin Multidisciplinary Health and Development Study (Dunedin Study) began in 1972 when the University of Otago Medical School, Dunedin, New Zealand began following the lives of 1037 children born between April 1972 and March 1973. The study is ongoing and has the support of governments and industry throughout the world.

Razor Films, 'When Teens Run off the Rails' (Season 1, Episode 2) [TV series episode], *Predict My Future: The Science of Us*, 2016.

Chapters 14, 44 and 52
Marianne Williamson, *A Return to Love: Reflections on the Principles of A Course in Miracles*, HarperCollins, 1992.

www.ingramcontent.com/pod-product-compliance
Lightning Source LLC
Chambersburg PA
CBHW050305010526
44107CB00055B/2109